Wolfsie in
Sheep's Clothing

How Life Pulls the Wool Over Your Eyes

Dick WOLFSIE

emmis
books

For further information, contact the publisher at:

books
Emmis Books
1700 Madison Road
Cincinnati, OH 45206

www.emmisbooks.com

Library of Congress Cataloging-in-Publication Data

Wolfsie, Dick.
  Wolfsie in sheep's clothing: how life pulls the wool over your eyes /
by Dick Wolfsie.
      p. cm.
  ISBN 1-57860-236-X
  1. American wit and humor. I. Title.
  PN6165.W64 2005
  814'.6--dc22
                                        2005008485

Interior designed by Mary Barnes Clark
Edited by Jessica Yerega
Cover designed by Pat Prather

To all those in my life who have recognized the magic of laughter, which does not include any of my elementary school teachers.

CONTENTS

Part 1

Baaah Humbug
(How We All Get a Good Fleecing)

36–30 or Fight 10
The Bridges of Hamilton County. 13
Being a Big Tipper 17
Food Fright 21
Getting an Inkling 24
Water on the Brain 28
The Fixer 31
One Angry Man 34
Something to Chew On 37
The Face of Food 41
My Main Squeeze 44
Dumb, Dumber, Dumbest 48
Card-Carrying Card Carrier 51
Spreading the News 54
Meet Right, Live Longer 58
Meat at Joe's 61
(Un)Fair Vacations 64
Wake-Up Hauls 67
Black Holes 70
Better Read This 73

Anger Management 76
Thought for Food 80
Price Hypes 84
Seals of Disapproval 87
Pig Tales 91
Movie Madness 94
Life-Changing Experience 97

Part 2

Sheepish Grins
(More RAMblings about Life)

Fishy Story 104
Good Morning? 107
Knows Cone 110
Fast Cash 113
Fat Chance of Success! 116
That's Debatable 119
Backing the Space Program 123
Missing Miss America 126
McDriver 130
Sick Humor 134
Mega-Bites 137
Heard of Cows 141

How to Read a Redhead 145

Cookie Monsters 148

Milk Duds 151

Take This Job and Love It 154

Pumped Up 157

My First McStep 160

Judging Poetry 163

Needs Improvement 167

Ants in the Pants 171

Part 3

Ewe and I

(Stories about My Flock)

Thought-Provoking 176

Have a Heart 179

Kernel of Truth 182

Deep Trouble 185

Waste Not, Want Not 188

Very Spatial Relationships 191

Safe at Home 194

Sonny Days 197

Meet the Napsters 200
Ghost of Christmas Present 203
My Son, the Spamster 206
Base Behavior 210
Being a Good Sport 213
Home Sweet Home 216
Calendar Girl 219

Part 4

*Shear*iously Speaking
(Gentle-as-a-Lamb Observations)

Record Comedy 224
Goodbye, Johnny 227
Respect the Comedian 230
Elephant Jokes 233
The Doctor Is "In" 237

Part 1

Baaah Humbug

(How We All Get a Good Fleecing)

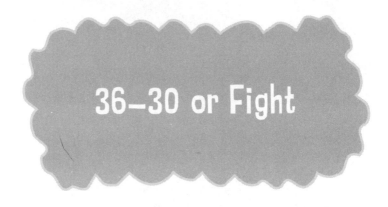

36–30 or Fight

Have you seen my pants lately?

I mean my 36–30 pants. That's not a brand name, like 501 jeans; that's my size. Yes, I have a 36-inch waist and two 30-inch legs. Now you know.

I am not proud of this. I didn't aspire to it (except when I was a 37). But I'm not unhappy with it either, although I'd rather be a 34.

Now, I ask you again. Have you seen my pants? No, not the ones I am wearing, although I'm beginning to think that they were the last 36–30s made in America. I'm looking for another pair of 36–30s. Where have all the 36–30s gone?

Every Saturday morning, I head out the door to look for pants. I'm either wearing my last pair of 36–30s, or I'm scrunched into 34–28s. Or waddling around in a pair of 38–32s.

First, I go to Ayres to look for pants. Man, do they have pants. And they have some really great sizes: 38–33, 42–28, 42–36, 40–34, 36–28. And that's just the beginning. The entire rack of clothes is a testimony to the myriad and wonderful ways that God works. Imagine creating humans in so many sizes!

But God, in his omnipotence, should have seen that making men with 36-inch waists and 30-inch legs was unnecessarily cruel. God should have known that 36–30 men would never find pants. Men like this are destined to be naked.

If God doesn't believe me, he's never been to Ayres, or Lazarus, or Kohl's. Even at Wal-Mart, where you can get kitty litter made for one cat, two cats, or multiple cats, I can't find 36–30 pants. Where are they all?

I look through the other sizes, hoping that some 36–30 who forgot his credit card may have squirreled away his size so he could return the next day and reclaim his treasure. Maybe there's a 36–30 in between the 44–30s and the 32–28s. That's where I once hid a pair of 36–30s. No luck. Let me tell you something: You can hide some of your income from the IRS in a bank in Switzerland, but you can't hide a pair of 36–30 pants. Trust me, I've tried.

So what is the explanation for this? Maybe the size is so rare that they don't manufacture very many. No way. True, you're more apt to see a 40–28 at the state fair or a 32–32 at the mini marathon, but I see 36–30s all day long: lawyers, doctors, plumbers, bus drivers. All 36–30, all apparently happy and well-adjusted. But I can see it in their eyes. And the way they walk. They can't find 36–30s either. It's so tragic.

The real explanation is that 36–30 is so common stores can't keep the size in stock. I know that when I see a pair of 40–29s, they are going to be there for a while. You see, men who are 40–29 won't admit it. They are probably trying to squeeze into my 36–30s. There oughtta be a law.

Some of you are saying to yourselves, "What a whiner." He's really a lucky guy. He doesn't have to go to the Small Man's Shop or the Big Man's Shop. His size is easy to find. He probably just double-parks his Suzuki in front of L.S. Ayres, runs in, grabs a 36–30 off the shelf, and is back in his car in five minutes.

In my dreams.

No one cares about 36–30s. We're a dime a dozen. We are normal around the middle, average from crotch to cuff. There is nothing distinctive about us. Except that we don't have any pants.

Of course, if you are a 48–30, or a 34–25, you probably read this entire essay and are now saying to yourself, "I don't find this whole thing very funny."

Well, neither do I.

The Bridges of Hamilton County

I'm not the kind of guy who sits in front of the TV all night and caresses the remote control, jumping from station to station, failing to watch any particular show for more than a few minutes. I'm not the kind of guy who just because I don't see a pretty girl or someone getting stabbed in the first thirty seconds zaps to another channel.

No, I am not just another one of those guys. I am THE guy. Everyone else is a pretender to the throne, a potato without a couch. Some people don't have a remote idea about anything. No one has more remote ideas than I do.

So you can imagine how excited I was when I went to get my teeth cleaned the other day and my hygienist slapped a shiny black remote in my hand, pointed to the TV, and stuck a probe into my gums.

This was too good to be true. Imagine watching *Law and Order* while slightly sedated, meaning I could see a rerun for the fourth time and be surprised by the ending!

I fumbled with the remote, knowing that my wife could not chastise me for channel surfing; my son could not castigate me for not stopping at the Discovery Channel. I had, indeed, found heaven during a routine six-month visit to the dental office.

I flipped on the power switch, eager to see how many channels my dentist had subscribed to, wondering if he had opted for satellite, cable, or dish. The man was a marketing genius. You can't learn this stuff in dental school.

The TV came on. I pressed menu, and gazed at my choices. It must have been a new service; I was unfamiliar with the programming:

- ROOT CANAL
- TMJ
- BRIDGES
- IMPLANTS
- TEETH WHITENING
- TONGUE PIERCING
- DENTURES

Oh joy! Channels I had never surfed, horizons I had never conquered, buttons I had never pushed. This was potentially more exciting than the Fish Bowl Channel or the Backgammon Channel. It almost, almost, made the Golf Channel look boring.

But there was more. Each channel had a submenu:

TEETH WHITENING
  1. Symptoms
  2. Diagnosis
  3. Treatment
  4. Prognosis
  5. Payment

Movies within movies, stories within stories—a concept made popular by Shakespeare and reintroduced by Dr. Smith of Noblesville, Indiana.

I clicked on "Treatment." Frightening close-ups of bad teeth filled the screen; visual effects crawled over the monitor, turning a horrid set of pearly grays into a string of Chiclets so breathtaking I was eager to see who the cinematographer was.

More close-ups—so close, in fact, that I never discovered who the actors and actresses were, but I know a good plot when I see one. Men and women who neglected their dental hygiene, destined to follow a path down the yellow-toothed road.

My session was almost over; time for only one more channel. I clicked on "BRIDGES." I prayed it wasn't some sappy love story about loneliness and isolation.

No, it was not *The Bridges of Madison County*. It was the Bridges of Hamilton County. There it was, right on the screen:

> # REAL PEOPLE
> # REAL STORIES
> # FAKE TEETH

I dared not weep, for fear my tears would suggest over-sensitivity of the teeth rather than the heart. As I started to get up from the chair, Dr. Smith bounded into the room.

"Dick, I just looked at your X-rays. You have a cavity on your right back molar. I'll need to fill it."

And so he did. Dr. Smith is a wonderful dentist. He did a great job filling my cavity. I can't wait for the movie.

Being a Big Tipper

A few weeks ago I had the pleasure of meeting Heloise, the hint guru who has a neat trick for every possible household problem. I like to think of Heloise as Martha Stewart without all the lawyers.

I was impressed to discover that she does exhaustive research on every tip she gets. And she gets hundreds—even thousands—every week. Her crack staff tests every single one, especially those sent by NAVE, The National Association of Vinegar Enthusiasts, which firmly believes that aspirin has been unfairly named the wonder drug and that people who consume vinegar only in salad dressing are kinda missing God's whole point for inventing the stuff in the first place.

The real mystery is the origin of some of these tips. Just the other day there was an article in the paper about how duct tape can reduce the amount of time it takes for warts to clear up. I was so annoyed at myself. For years, I've been wrapping my warts with Scotch tape, masking tape, and electrical tape, but I never tried duct tape. What was I thinking?

So how do people make these discoveries in the first place? What prompts a person to wrap his head in duct tape? And once he does, how can someone that stupid then be smart enough to realize two weeks later that there's some connection between that and his fading warts? Millions of years ago, people figured out there was a connection between having sex and having babies nine months later. I guess this duct tape thing pales in comparison.

Someone told me they read in the paper that if you soak olive pits in red wine and dog urine for two hours and place them in your basement it will keep rats away. Don't you just want to smack yourself in the head and say, "Now why didn't I think of that? It's so obvious."

Even more frustrating is when you read in the newspaper that if you soak a Brillo pad in vodka and Mountain Dew and nail it to a tree in your backyard, it will keep the deer from eating your bushes. "I've been doing that for years," you say. "And now someone else is making money on my ideas."

These things happen every day in America.

"Shirley!"

"Yes, Harold."

"Have you noticed how much healthier my complexion looks these past few weeks?"

"Yes, you look totally vibrant, Harold. How do you account for that?"

"Well, the last month or so I've been wearing your pantyhose to bed to keep warm."

"Well, that must be it. What else could it be?"

"Well, I did change from a scrubby pad to a sponge to wash my face."

"Now, Harold, how could that make a difference? No, it's the pantyhose. Better write Heloise."

Here are some rejected tips. Don't try 'em, just laugh at 'em.

- If you sleep with a jar of green olives for two weeks, it will cure your arthritis. And make it easier to have a martini first thing in the morning.

- If you spray your dog's tongue with a mixture of soy sauce, pumpkin juice, and vinegar, you will hear him bark less. Because he will run away.

- Instead of floor wax, try mixing banana puree and nail polish remover. You can also use this to clean your whitewall tires or poison a monkey.

- For doors that stick, try a mixture of prune juice and castor oil. Wait a second, I may be confusing this with another problem.

That's enough advice for today. My wife wants me to fix the torn screen. Maybe I can borrow Harold's pantyhose.

Food Fright

USA Today reported last week on the ten most dangerous foods you can eat while driving. Accidents that occur while munching on these delicacies are called food-related wrecks. Just when you finally realize that holding a cell phone to your ear while reading a newspaper and making a U-turn is dangerous, now it appears that eating a taco can be just as deadly.

Fasten your seat belts—loosely—and listen to this: A group of scientists did extensive research into food-related accidents by getting in their SUVs and driving around hairpin turns while trying to eat Kentucky Fried Chicken. Apparently, it isn't the ninety grams of fat that kills you, or smacking into a pylon. It's parallel parking while licking your fingers.

The research lasted two years. Fortunately, there were no traffic deaths, but the twenty-five researchers gained a combined six hundred pounds, and ruined four leather seat covers and sixty pairs of polyester pants.

The number one most dangerous food, by the way, was coffee. Piping hot coffee in the lap proved to be a distraction to almost everyone who had any kind of personal life when they got home. Most people kept their hands on the wheel when the coffee spilled, but they cracked their heads wide open when they hit the roof and yelled something that sounded like Curly of the Three Stooges.

Hot soup was next. I don't know about you, but there's nothing better than a hot cup of cream of broccoli soup while driving to work in the morning. I manage it pretty well, but my wife insists I use a spoon. I think that's even more dangerous. In several cases, it wasn't spilling the soup that caused the distraction, but sprinkling on the croutons.

Number three was tacos. According to the research, tacos crumble easily and people try to catch the falling pieces, leaving no hands on the wheel. The police in California are really cracking down on this and they now have a Taco Breathalyzer Test. Fail it, and they put you in a Tijuana slammer with an annoying little Chihuahua named Pancho.

Number four was called "chili-covered food." This causes accidents because women immediately try to blot the stain, while men bend over and try to lick the chili off their pants.

As I mentioned earlier, fried chicken was studied, and it made the list at number seven. But here's the good news: grilled chicken, chicken piccata, chicken Florentine, chicken francaise—none of those made the list. Enjoy.

Number eight was jelly doughnuts. I'm sorry, but if you can't eat a Krispy Kreme and drive safely on I-465, you should get a home office. By the way, jelly doughnuts were more dangerous than cream-filled. Good news if you are fighting both traffic and high cholesterol.

Number nine was soft drinks. Apparently, accidents are caused by people looking down so they can get the cup into the holder. Dr Pepper was more dangerous than Coke, but Mountain Dew was the most dangerous soft drink of all. Like you didn't know that.

The least dangerous food of the top ten was chocolate, but it still rated a potential threat. The researchers considered a Mounds candy bar the equivalent in danger to a high-speed blowout. Sometimes it takes a PhD to take the fun out of candy.

This is serious business. If you want to pig out in your car after barreling through a Wendy's or McDonald's drive-through, consider climbing in the back seat to chow down. Then get a friend to drive.

Don't think of yourself as a glutton; think of yourself as a designated eater.

Getting an Inkling

I've been in a snit all week about ink. That's right,
ink. You see, I bought this machine, this high-tech
computer printer that does just about everything.
It prints photos, creates greeting cards, addresses
envelopes, does spreadsheets, sends faxes, makes copies.
I swear it could defrost lasagna if I gave it a chance.

The cost? One hundred dollars.

Imagine that: one hundred dollars. What a deal. So
what put me in a snit? The ink for this computer, this
tiny vial of black stuff that is probably worth about
eighty cents, cost me thirty dollars. That's 30 dollars,
$30. No matter how I write it, it's thirty bucks. XXX
bucks to you people in Rome.

Where do they get this stuff from? A rare squid?

Thirty bucks for ink. But once you buy the printer,
they have you by the cartridges by making you buy

the cartridges. (Read that last line again. Very funny!)

While I detest this little scam, I must admit that it is a bit of marketing genius. What I see in the future is unscrupulous corporate executives (excuse the redundancy) using this technique to sell other products. My advice: Be sure to read the fine print.

FIVE-BEDROOM HOME, $79,500

That's right. Five bedrooms, three-car garage, swimming pool, and tennis court. Your gorgeous front lawn, grown from a rare Chinese grass seed, requires a special fertilizer each month, available only through our company. Cost: $350 per month.

MICROWAVE OVEN, ONLY $3.50

(Will only microwave our specially made frozen dinners, available for $14.95 each. Serves up to one person.)

NEW CARS STARTING AT $295

Drive the car of your dreams for less than $300. Includes leather seats, CD player. Requires special gas: $4.50 a gallon, available only at our dealership service stations.

PEDIGREE FRENCH POODLE COMPLETE WITH SHOTS, $1.50

Our poodles only eat our specially formulated dog food ($130 a pound). This week's special: dog biscuits, $24.50 each.

NOT A DOG LOVER? HOW ABOUT A RARE CARABELLIAN CAT?

The cat is only $1.75. Has all its shots, and we'll deliver it for free. Note: Carabellian cats only use a special imported clay kitty litter, otherwise say goodbye to your living room carpet. Carabellian Cat Litter is $79 a box (scoop included).

THE GOOD KNIGHT BED ONLY $1.49

It's not a king-size bed, not a queen-size bed. It's a knight size. Just perfect for many modern bedrooms. And we make the only sheets that fit this bed: $650 for a fitted bottom. The top sheets are on us. So to speak.

RUSSIAN WIVES FOR SALE

For $7, we'll fly your beautiful Russian wife to America. These eager young women will meet your every desire. Note: Our Russian women will only sleep on the Good Knight Bed (see above). And they want new sheets every month, or goodbye romance.

MOVIE TICKETS ONLY $7.50

For a mere $7.50, you can see a major Hollywood production featuring the hottest motion picture stars in the world. Enjoy a large popcorn and a soft drink for $11.50. NOTE TO READERS: This is already true, in case you haven't been to the movies lately.

ANOTHER NOTE TO READERS: This essay is free, but you have to buy the book.

Water on the Brain

I'm not the smartest consumer in the world, but the other day when I was scanning the label on my bottled water to make sure there were no carbs in it, I saw something strange. "Best if drunk by December 31, 2006." Well, that's New Year's Eve, and I am at my best if I'm drunk before the year changes, but I don't think that's what they mean.

That gave me just two years to gulp down the product, or else. Or else what?

I think it's fair to ask what is actually going to happen to this water after two years. It can't lose its nutrient value. It doesn't have any. It can't lose its color. It has none.

One company I spoke to said the water changes in taste after a year. Changes to what? I sure wouldn't know. With a bag of Doritos and a jar of Redd Foxx

Salsa, I can't tell the difference between Budweiser and Maplehurst Farms.

And so what if my Evian tastes funny? There's a world of difference between funny-tasting water and funny-tasting mayonnaise. Trust me.

What about people who buy bottled water for the sole purpose of storing it in case of a terrorist attack?

"Harold, I have some bad news for you. We've been hiding in the basement now for two months and I think our bottled water has expired."

"Pour it down the drain, Maude. I know how little willpower you have when you get dehydrated."

Then I read that the American Red Cross advises changing your bottled water every six months. I doubt I'll remember. I haven't changed my tartar sauce in thirteen years. There is a jar of honey in my pantry that I took with me when I hiked to the bottom of the Grand Canyon in 1969.

I also have cheese in the fridge that has been aged twelve years, but when I brought it home, the package said there was only a month left to eat it. I say, "Age it eleven years. Give me the extra twelve months."

So what should you do with this expired water? You can't just pour it down your kitchen sink. There's probably some government regulation against it. With my luck, I'll end up buying property next to an expired water dump. There go the real estate values.

By the way, I checked my cans of Pepsi and 7UP.

There are no expiration dates. I think this is great news for anthropologists of the future. When they dig up my remains in a frozen block of ice, I'll be knocking down a Fresca, my diet libation of choice.

"Dr. Gallagher, this ancient man we found with the Channel 8 ball cap has something called a Fresca in his hand. Looks like some kind of prehistoric drink. I think the drink is four thousand years old. Can we taste it?

"Is there an expiration date on the can?"

"No, professor. No expiration date."

"Go for it. Just be sure it's not pure water."

I know we are all going to die, but I'm glad people don't have expiration dates printed on them. Although, at the age of fifty-seven, mine should probably read: BEST IF USED BY DECEMBER 2035.

The Fixer

I have a fix-it guy who doesn't fix things. Then how do I even know he is a fix-it guy, you ask? This is very existential, but try to follow me. He could fix things if he wanted to, but he chooses not to. This is what made George Washington so special. It wasn't that Washington couldn't tell a lie. George was a clever chap; he would have been very good at lying. He just chose not to.

There's a lot of George Washington in Steve.

When Steve comes over, we sit and talk about his kids and his grandkids. Then he gets around to his infirmities and then his wife's aches and pains. Then what's new at the temple. And finally, how things are going at his regular job. Which, interestingly, is just talking to people on the phone about their problems. And he's not a therapist—he's an acoustical engineer.

Then it's time for a little lunch. We talk about the history of smoked salmon, the relative merits of a Kosher hot dog, and the debate about yellow vs. brown mustard.

Then we start talking about his granddaughter, Amanda, again. Apparently she is a very good talker for only a two-year-old. This trait must run in the family.

After about an hour, I do something that is a bit rude. I ask Steve about actually fixing something. Like the door that won't close properly.

"Steve, sorry to interrupt, but can we talk about fixing the hinge on the front door?"

I think I should be more careful how I phrase things because for the next hour, that's exactly what we do. Or, to be more accurate, that's what Steve does. Last week I learned a lot about the long and rich history of the door hinge, the benefits of stainless steel over iron, the evolution of the pin that allows the hinge to move freely. And the best type of oil to use. It was very interesting. Yeah, right.

But my door still didn't close.

"I'll have to fix that hinge another time," said Steve. "It's getting late."

"It wasn't late when you got here six hours ago."

"Dick, these things take time. What's a good day for me to come back?"

"Why are you coming back? Can't we just do this over the phone?"

Steve returned a week later. He would have come back sooner, but he was very busy and had a lot of people he needed to talk to.

"Hi. Is the door still broken?"

"Well, of course it's still broken. You didn't fix it."

"I know, but we talked for almost an hour. It still won't close?"

Finally, Steve got out his tool box and began working....

"Excuse me, Steve, but that is not the door that's broken."

"If you're so good at fixing things, why don't you do it?"

"I bet I could, if I wanted to."

"Dick, I think you're all talk."

"So are you. But that's at thirty dollars an hour."

"Talk is not cheap, Dick."

I am in no position to argue with Steve, the fix-it man. Right now in my house, I have a broken door, a busted window, a dishwasher on the fritz, a bad electric socket, a computer that is making weird sounds, and a blown fuse that I can't find.

No, I'm not going to tick off Steve, the fix-it man. We have a lot to talk about.

One Angry Man

I'm a pretty even-tempered guy. But this week just about everything that happened to me ticked me off. I have been told not to sweat the small things, but it's the small things that drive me nuts. Big things, I have no control over. But give me a small thing and I get this crazy idea that I can actually do something about it. That's enough to drive a man crazy.

I'm going to mention a few of those things, and it would mean a great deal to me if you'd go over to your computer and e-mail me and let me know if you agree. My e-mail is wolfsie@aol.com. I'm serious about this. Just knowing I'm not alone would mean the world to me.

Okay, it's been such a rotten week, I'm not sure where to begin. How about this letter I got in the mail from my storage facility:

Dear Mr. Wolfsie,

In order to continue to provide you with the quality service you have come to expect, we are raising your monthly rate from thirty-five dollars to forty dollars.

EXCUUUSE ME!!! Quality service? What service? It's a closet, next to four hundred other closets. I put stuff in the box MYSELF. I clean the closet; I rearrange the closet; I throw out stuff; I put in new stuff. They do NOTHING. There's only one person who works in the entire place. What's her job? She sends out notices telling you your rates are going up.

Here's another annoyance: I don't want the checkout people at Sam's Club calling me by my first name after they look at my card. Truth is, I love it when everyone calls me Dick. But when I go to Sam's Club, some eighteen-year-old kid looks at my Club Card and says, "Thanks, Richie." RICHIE?? Who in Sam Wal-Mart is Richie? I don't want to be called by my first name in line at Sam's Club. If you see me in a restaurant or on the street, please call me Dick. If you take my money at Sam's Club, I prefer Mr. Wolfsie. If you call me Richie anywhere, I'll lock you in my storage closet.

And another: My waiter the other night at a very nice restaurant introduced himself and said he would be our ambassador for the evening. HELLO! You're my *what*? Look, I don't want an ambassador. I want a waiter. It's hard enough getting another beer from a waiter, but throw some international politics into this and I could be alcohol-free the rest of my life.

One more: There are people in my neighborhood who still have their Christmas decorations up. I'm trying to gear up for spring and forget the snowiest winter in Indiana history, and the Fabershams have a Christmas wreath on their door and a tree in their living room. It gets worse. They actually turn the lights on. I can forgive someone who is too busy to pack up the holiday stuff, but when you make a conscious effort to put on the lights, you're looking for a post-Noel fight. There's a part of me that just wants to dress up like a leprechaun, knock on the door March 17, and introduce them to a new holiday. And while I'm at the door, I think I'll crush the jack-o-lantern on their porch. I'm tired of that, also.

There are a few other things that ticked me off this week: high gas prices, Osama bin Laden, North Korea's nuclear weapons, and terrorism. I'd complain about those as well, but I don't want to look petty.

Something to Chew On

There is big news in the world of candy. Researchers now claim that a compound derived from licorice root may help slow the effects of aging on the brain and keep mental skills sharp. The research went on to say that eating licorice daily will stop you from losing your memory as you get older.

In a nutshell, here are some additional findings. Licorice is purported to:

Control respiratory problems and soothe a sore throat. Lessen symptoms of chronic fatigue syndrome and fibromyalgia. Combat hepatitis. Calm skin irritations such as eczema and shingles. Treat PMS and menstrual problems. Prevent heart disease. Fight cancer. Alleviate ulcers, heartburn, indigestion, and inflammatory bowel problems such as Crohn's disease and ulcerative colitis.

WOW!

And as of today, you can buy licorice over the counter—the candy counter, that is. No prescription needed. But that will all change if Eli Lilly can figure out a way to get those rubbery sticks into a tiny plastic bottle. If that happens and licorice is officially declared a drug, the cost will soar and might even exceed what you pay in the movie theater. Then the government will require warnings on the bottle:

LICORICE Side effects include: blackened teeth, reddened teeth, no teeth, inflamed gums, jaw ache, weight gain, funny facial expressions when chewing, sudden death. Do not eat licorice if you plan to operate heavy machinery, drive a car, or ride a tricycle. In rare cases, licorice may cause impotence, but findings are inconclusive because most of the people eating licorice are under seven years old.

By the way, don't worry about that sudden death part. They always throw that in in case you're eating licorice while you're talking on your cell phone and trying to make a left-hand turn.

Eating licorice, as suggested in the warning, could lead to tooth loss, which is very ironic because most of the people who have eaten licorice their entire lives still have very vivid memories of the fun they had when they had their own choppers. There's a downside to everything.

When I read about the therapeutic value of licorice, I called my wife at work. She has always been a little concerned about memory loss and I wanted her to hear the good news....

"Hello, Mary Ellen."

"HrdtotlknwIhvlicrcinmymth."

"Well, sounds like you already heard the news."

"HMMM?"

"I hope you're eating the red licorice. Black licorice has just the opposite effect."

"UH OH."

I now understand there is one university doing nothing but sugar-related research, desperately seeking indisputable data that all candies have some therapeutic benefit, thus providing solace to those who have been previously handicapped by their sweet tooth.

This is the kind of research I have always wanted to do. Not as researcher, but as researchee. Unfortunately, most of this testing is being done with animals. Normally animals are opposed to scientific research, but being fed Hershey bars, Tootsie Rolls, and Bit-O-Honeys is a step up from being forced to smoke three packs of cigarettes a day.

Word has it that hamsters, guinea pigs, and rats are

lined up every morning at the research center looking for work. But the screening process involves eating a string of licorice in under two minutes without having to sit in the corner of the cage and pick their teeth for the rest of the day.

This is probably the dumbest essay I have ever written. But someday it will just be forgotten history. It will be for me, anyway. I hate licorice.

The Face
of Food

A woman from Hollywood, Florida, made the news when she revealed that ten years ago she was eating a grilled cheese sandwich and saw the image of the Virgin Mary in the bread. She sold the item on eBay for twenty-eight thousand dollars. She claimed it was whole wheat, but you gotta figure it was Wonder Bread.

There is very little information about the buyer. In fact, no one is even sure if he is very religious or if he just loves cheese that's been aged a full decade, which, as you know, can get pretty pricey.

The very same story reports that when the woman made this supernatural discovery, she put the sandwich in a clear plastic box with cotton balls and placed it on her dresser for ten years. I'm no social historian, but I think the old cotton ball theory of food preservation is pretty outdated. I'm guessing that after two, three months, that sandwich was pretty much history.

I am not criticizing this woman's religious beliefs. I just have to wonder why the forces responsible for this miracle would choose a grilled cheese sandwich. The Lord has revealed himself in some glorious ways, but a grilled cheese sandwich pales in comparison to a burning bush.

Why does stuff like this never happen to me? I've been staring at my lunch for fifty years and the most I ever saw, maybe, was a very faint profile of Walter Matthau in an egg salad sandwich on rye, which I have been told would have gone for two bucks on eBay, assuming I got the sandwich to the buyer while it was still edible. Pumpernickel? You're looking at $2.50.

After I read about this story, I started paddling through my wife's beef stew but with little success. Then I bought a package of frozen vegetables at Marsh and when I opened it up I thought, for a brief moment, that I saw Jeff Gordon in the carrot, cauliflower, and green bean medley. But once the glob started to thaw, it honestly could have been any race-car driver. So I just ate it.

I do believe you can find celebrity images in Jell-O, but once what I thought was Pat Sajak and Vanna White in the cherry-flavored variety was just my own reflection with my wife standing behind me, laughing.

The problem with a story like this is that people who are looking for a quick buck on eBay will start imagining these culinary apparitions. It's one thing to look into the clouds and see Mickey Mouse; it's quite another to start telling people you saw Jessica Simpson in your eggplant parmagiana.

For many years, Myrtle Young of Fort Wayne has amassed a collection of potato chips that resemble celebrities like Snoopy, George Bush, and Yogi Bear. She recently complained that she's been having a heck of a time finding new additions. Her daughter, who supplies her with chips, had been substituting with Pringles from the Dollar Store.

Well, that's it for this column. My wife ordered a pepperoni and sausage pizza for dinner and it just arrived. I'm not really hungry, but it's fun to see new people.

My Main Squeeze

I am the juice man.

I love juice. All kinds of juice. But don't confuse me with the guy on TV who is about eighty-five years old and is hawking some juicemaker machine. He says that because he drinks juice every day, he has just fathered triplets and now has a slew of toddlers running around the house. Personally, this would not be a motivating factor for me to drink juice when I become an octogenarian. In fact, I'm going to lay off the juice starting when I'm eighty-three. I'm not taking any chances. And even though my wife will be seventy-nine, I'm taking the V8 away from her also.

I can't just drink juice plain, however. I am a compulsive mixer. Orange and guava, grapefruit and mango, strawberry and lemonade, grape and tangerine. I've mixed lemonade and grape, cranberry and peach, apple and raspberry. Sometimes I'll combine three or four juices. And I don't buy juices already mixed. I do it myself. I'm some exciting guy, aren't I?

Every combination is more delectable than the last. Each one chock-full of vitamin C. I haven't had a cold in fifty years.

My long association with juice has made me a keen observer of some fruit juice conundrums. Let me share them with you:

1. Why is there no raisin juice? There is prune juice, which is from dried-up plums. Why not raisin juice? Just dried-up grapes.

2. Why is there no plum juice? Sounds good to me.

3. Where has all the pineapple juice gone? I can't find it in any store. Is someone buying up all the pineapple juice? Don't tell me you buy pineapple juice in little cans. That doesn't count. Do you buy beer in little tiny cans? I don't think so.

4. How come apple juice has 100 percent vitamin C, but on an apple cider label it says there is no vitamin C. Where did the vitamin C go?

5. If vegetable juice is fat free, why is vegetable

oil 100 percent fat? I've been asking that question for ten years and still haven't gotten an answer I like.

6. How come there is no cantaloupe juice? Cantaloupes are just waiting to be squeezed. They are full of juice. It's cruel and inhuman, like not milking a cow.

7. Does white grape juice stain like the blue grape juice, but you just can't see the stain? (This will keep you up all night, so don't think about it too much.)

8. Why does orange juice in a can taste like grapefruit juice? Trust me, it does.

9. Why can't I get grape juice with pulp?

10. Why did lemonade become such a hit? Who handled the PR for limeade, anyway?

11. If orange juice is 100 percent juice, then what is concentrate? 500 percent juice?

12. Why does a lemon cost a quarter, but when you add water and sugar to make lemonade, it costs three dollars at the state fair? I will tell you

why: It's the best drink in America, that's why! By the way, lemonade in a can is vile. Lemonade from powder should be illegal. Frozen lemonade? Not bad. Not bad at all.

13. Some orange juice has no pulp. I like pulp. What did they do with the pulp? I wouldn't mind buying some extra pulp. I'd put it in my grape juice.

14. Why is all grape juice from concentrate? You can buy fresh orange juice and fresh grapefruit juice. But no fresh grape juice. I'd sure love to know why. I mean, wine isn't from concentrate. Hey, there's an idea....

15. And finally, I want to know why I can't buy pure cranberry juice. It's always in some kind of cocktail. I think that should be my decision. After all, I AM THE JUICE MAN.

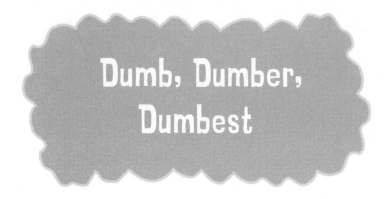

Dumb, Dumber, Dumbest

As I look back on the past year (2004), I would like to report on the three dumbest ideas I have read about. You may have your own, but these are my favorites.

First, Dumb:

The NFL has just decided to put luxury throne-like seats on the sidelines at Gillette Stadium in Foxboro, Massachusetts. They want the fans to feel more like part of the game.

I think this is a wonderful idea because after the NBA melee in Detroit, there was some concern that the athletes had to travel too far to punch the fans—so the players' union is advocating seats right on the field. This is also beneficial to the fans who have been complaining that if they are going to be assaulted, they'd like to just get it over with, go to the emergency room, and be home in time for Jerry Springer reruns.

Scott Suprima, who works for Seating Solutions, designed the seats and admits that they may have to construct a canopy to protect the patrons who paid big bucks for this option. Suprima's company was concerned that people in the luxury seats might be mistaken for athletes by people in the cheap seats and get hit by a chair.

By the way, according to *USA Today*, there will also be plasma TVs next to the seats, which I am assuming is for blood transfusions.

Now, Dumber:

There is a new government regulation stating that you are not allowed to smile when having your passport or driver's license photo taken: As it was described in the newspaper, "the machine can be flummoxed by smiles, which introduce teeth, wrinkles, seams, and other distortions."

First of all, I never thought of my smile as introducing my teeth. I usually just say hello to people. If they want to get friendly with my teeth, they'll just have to make their own introductions.

And as far as wrinkles go, we all have them. Seams, I'm not so sure about. What is a seam? I've always thought of my face as pretty seamless, but I want to thank the U.S. government for giving me yet another thing to worry about since September 11, 2001.

Plus, it ticked me off I had to look up "flummoxed" in the dictionary.

Of course, once again we have another silly, unnecessary regulation. I've been to the Bureau of Motor Vehicles hundreds of times and I have never seen people voluntarily smiling to begin with. In fact, if you ask people to smile for their BMV photo, they'll rant for twenty minutes on why they can't think of anything to be happy about. Then they'll take a ticket and sit for another two hours waiting for the picture.

And as far as passports are concerned, remember the words of Mark Twain: If you look like your passport photo, you're probably too sick to travel.

Dumbest:

And finally, the dumbest idea of the year. Airlines are thinking about letting people use cell phones on airplanes. If they can ban nail clippers, they should ban cell phones. I'd rather sit next to a man clipping his toenails than a woman talking on her cell phone to her boyfriend in Chicago.

But with my luck, next time I'll be sitting right between them.

Card-Carrying Card Carrier

I have always wanted to collect something no one else collected.

Actually, that's kinda dumb because if you're the only one collecting something, you won't get a monthly newsletter. And there's no one to brag to when you finally find whatever is that you've been looking for to complete your collection. And if your collection is really valuable, there's no one to sell it to. Come to think of it, if no one collects what you collect, it won't be valuable anyway. WOW, I sure talked myself out of that idea, didn't I?

The other day I was at the car wash. I spent some time looking at state-of-the-art polyester sun visors and all the concoctions that make your car smell new (which is stupid in a car that's fifteen years old). But I didn't look at the floor mats. I stopped using them years ago. Seems to me that with floor mats you have to clean both the floor and the mats. I only have to clean the floor in my car. I can't be the first person to have figured this out.

But I digress.

The Sparkling Image Car Wash also has a great assortment of greeting cards—cards that are funnier, I might add, than your average Hallmark selection. I think people need a good laugh when both they and their cars are getting soaked for twenty bucks.

Many of the cards had cartoons of political figures. I counted twenty-five different ones, replete with caricatures and satirical remarks about George Bush, John Kerry, Bill and Hillary Clinton, Dick Cheney, and Al Gore. Apparently there is nothing funny about John Edwards. Go figure.

There were also cards with Bob Dole (when he did those Viagra commercials, he was just asking for it) and even today, there are more Dan Quayle cards than you can shake a potato (potatoe?) at.

When I got home, I went on the Internet to find out how far back the idea of funny political greeting cards went. I wanted to research a little of their history.

I Yahooed, I Googled—but I found nothing. How strange is that?

I called my friend, Mike McQuillen, one of the top political button collectors in the country. I asked him about the history of these cards.

"Not a clue, Dick."

Certainly a political cartoonist would know. I called two.

"No idea, Dick."

"No idea, Dick."

A political science professor at Indiana University?

"Sorry, I never thought about it. And please don't use my name in your story."

Was it possible I had found something that no one else collected? You can go online and find people who collect sugar packets, manhole covers, fruit jars, and water sprinklers. But apparently no one collects political greeting cards. Just what I was looking for!

So there you have it. I am now officially a collector of funny political greeting cards. I am up to twenty-five of them.

And I hate to brag, but I have the biggest collection in the world.

Spreading the News

Can we talk about condiments? As we get older, the taste buds just don't seem to have quite the zip that they used to. This makes mustard, ketchup, and even bland old mayonnaise very important to the aging population.

I'd include tartar sauce, but you don't see a great deal of tartar sauce nowadays. You probably have had a jar in your fridge for years. Open it up. If it smells funny, it's probably still okay.

I'm actually surprised that I haven't written about condiments before. I haven't ever mentioned French's or Heinz or Gulden's in any of my stories. Considering my near obsession with condiments, this seems impossible.

Condiments must generally be a male thing. You would never hear a man say to his wife, "Golly, with all that ketchup on the burger, Sweetheart, you can't possibly appreciate the fine texture and flavor of the grain-fed beef." Women, on the other hand, are more apt to say, "If you put ketchup on my chicken Kiev, I will rip your ruby-red tongue right out of your mouth."

Of all the condiments, mustard still has my vote for tastiest. I did some research on the Internet and discovered that there are about one hundred different kinds of mustard, but basically, there is only one kind of ketchup. There are gourmet mustards—mustards you would gently brush on a seventy-five-dollar rack of lamb—but there is no gourmet ketchup that I am aware of. I would welcome a good gourmet ketchup. I think most Hoosiers would. Somebody is missing a golden opportunity here. I know you're still kicking yourself for not thinking of designer water first, so don't let this gourmet ketchup thing get away.

I don't want to brag, but I have improved just about every dinner my wife has ever prepared by carefully adding the appropriate condiment.

What would her chicken marsala be like without my mayonnaise? Uneventful, that's what. How would her beef Bourguignon taste without mustard? I shudder to think. And what about her veal Oscar without ketchup? Lifeless. And I'm being generous.

Here's some final advice:

1. You can leave mustard and ketchup on your dining room table overnight and still put it safely back in the fridge the next day. Don't do this with mayonnaise. There is an entire cemetery in Brooklyn, New York, filled with people who hid a pastrami sandwich from their spouse, putting it under the bed and then forgetting that Russian dressing is half mayonnaise.

2. When placing mustard on a sandwich, ALWAYS put the mustard in between the meats on the bread. Mayonnaise, however, needs to go on the top of the meat. Ketchup can go either way. Never apply condiments directly to the bread. This information is the result of a grant by the U.S. government to a national taste-testing institute. Finally, tax money well spent.

3. Turn upside down and shake all plastic bottles vigorously before squeezing mustard or ketchup on your sandwich. Nevertheless, the bottle will still make an embarrassing sound. If you want a laugh from your kids, just say "excuse me" after it squirts. It's foolproof.

4. NEVER buy mayonnaise in a squeeze bottle. Mayonnaise belongs in a glass jar. Buying mayonnaise in a plastic squeeze bottle would be like

buying whipped cream in a box. It's not normal. It's un-American. The manufacturers should be arrested. Where is the FBI when you really need them? Probably at the airport.

5. I think it is important that kids learn about ketchup, mayonnaise, and mustard at home. I don't want the public school system passing out condiments in the cafeteria. I think it should be up to the parents.

Meet Right,
Live Longer

Ever notice how difficult it is to meet people nowadays? Oh, I don't mean "meet" in the romantic sense. I mean find a place to meet. You know, have a meeting.

When I was a kid living just outside of New York City, the coolest thing to do was meet in the Big Apple. The place to meet was under the clock at Grand Central Station. This, of course, was where everyone met. On some days, it seemed that some six or eight million people were crammed under the clock looking for their friends and lovers and drug dealers. Still today, you can find the occasional New Yorker searching under the clock for a loved one they've been missing since the early '60s.

The thing about the clock is that there was never any question what you meant. If you did ask which clock, there was good chance you were a spy or an illegal immigrant. It was like saying, "Now which Empire State Building did you mean?"

When I was teaching high school back in the suburbs of New York, we'd all meet at Leo's Deli. If you said, "See you at Leo's," there was little question where to go. The big question was: pastrami on rye or corned beef on rye?

But things have changed.

I was meeting my friend David for coffee the other day at a favorite restaurant, Le Peep. Le Peep—in case you are not familiar with the place—is to eggs what Marlene Dietrich, Betty Grable, and Mary Hart are to legs. This is not a perfect analogy, but it does explain my low score on the verbal SATs. Notice that I was sensitive to my readers, embracing lovely gams from several different generations. Man, am I off the subject.

Back to David. He was late. Where was he? He'd never been late before. When I asked the cashier, she suggested he might have gone to a different Le Peep.

"Does that happen often?" I asked.

"Oh yes. You see, we have four Le Peeps. In fact three of them are on 86th street, but they're several miles apart."

"Well, that was great planning. Could you call and see if he went to a different one?

"Which one?"

"Well, if I knew which one, you can just bet I would have gone directly there."

I decided I never wanted this to happen again so when another friend called and suggested we meet at Starbucks for coffee, I was on top of it. By the way, I don't generally go to Starbucks for coffee. Meeting at Starbucks for coffee is like meeting a friend at the movie theater for a Diet Sprite and a bag of popcorn. This is a good idea if you are looking to spend $8.50 for a drink that has no food value and a bag of air containing eighty-five grams of fat.

"Which Starbucks?" I asked. I'm no dummy.

There was dead silence. This is not an easy question. Five years ago, it was a no-brainer.

"Okay, how about the Starbucks next to Panera Bread?" she suggested.

"Which Panera Bread? The one next to the Wal-Mart or the one next to Marsh?"

"The one next to Marsh!"

"The Marsh next to the Cingular Wireless or the Marsh next to Sprint?

"The Marsh next to Cingular Wireless."

"The one next to Denny's or the one..."

I could go on with this forever. In fact, I did go on forever in my first draft, but then my wife said it was very quickly not getting any funnier, which is a bizarre sentence that has a number of grammatical and syntactical problems, but it certainly was clear what she meant.

If you don't get my point, I'll explain it to you in person. Meet me at noon tomorrow at Wendy's.

Meat at Joe's

I read the other day that theme restaurants, the craze of the '90s, may be having a resurgence. Does that mean that somewhere along the line, they lost their surge? Theme restaurants, like Planet Hollywood, sold delicious T-shirts. Too bad their hamburgers tasted like 50 percent cotton and 50 percent polyester.

I hate theme restaurants. You go to an eatery called the Ship Ahoy and all the waitresses are dressed like mermaids, the waiters have a patch on one eye, and you have to drink your beer out of a conch shell. The menu, of course, is on a paddle, which can get pretty dangerous. In some cases, they actually have fish on the menu.

Hooters is a theme restaurant, I guess. But the part of the chicken they specialize in is wings. I think that's a big marketing mistake.

In many restaurants, the bathroom doors reflect the theme. At the racetrack restaurant, I know I'm a stud (no problem there) and not a filly. But setters or pointers threw me at the Bird Dog Inn, and I'm sorry, but am I an enchilada or a tamale at Pedro's Mexican restaurant? At a seafood restaurant's restrooms, I chose shark over barracuda. I remembered an old co-host of mine so I got lucky.

And while I am in a snit about this: I don't want my menu on a football, a baseball glove, or a bowling ball. I saw the other day where there is a new chain of restaurants with a computer theme. I know the menus will be on floppy disks. I won't eat there if the appetizers are called MINI BYTES. I wouldn't be surprised if they called the waiters SERVERS. Well, I guess that's okay. I do have some sense of humor, you know.

Hey, why not a hospital-themed restaurant? Hospitals are always looking for a new way to market their services.

"Hello, Mr. Wolfsie! Welcome to Isle de Pancreas Restaurant. If you'll have a seat in our waiting room, we'll beep you when the waiter can see you. If the wait is too long, we suggest that you yell out 'We're dying of hunger.' It won't help, but it makes things more realistic."

We waited forever. My wife was annoyed because I kept looking at the young waitresses. I loved their uniforms, especially how they opened down the back.

We were finally seated and our drinks were served. "Mr. Wolfsie," said the waitress, "Don't you like your wine?"

"I guess so. I've never sipped merlot from an intravenous tube before."

"I hope it's the type you like. Get it? The *type* you like? Just a little hospital joke. Here are your menus."

"On a bed pan?"

"Oh, yes, our customers love that homey touch. I just wish people wouldn't sit on them. We don't find that funny anymore."

The meal arrived. It was tasteless. They had taken the hospital theme a bit too far. Suddenly, the waiter rushed in.

"Sir, there has been a terrible mistake. We gave you someone else's liver."

"That's okay, I don't mind."

"Sir, we can't afford a malpreparation suit. You might enjoy it now, but reject it later tonight. Why don't you ask your wife what she thinks. We always encourage a second opinion."

"How about another glass of water? I don't know why I'm so thirsty."

"We get a lot of that, sir. People are not used to wiping their mouths with a gauze pad."

"Look, this place is crazy. Can I have a check? Do you take Visa or Master Card?"

"Sorry, neither. Only Blue Cross or Blue Shield."

(Un)Fair Vacations

There should be some law about starting school during the state fair. I don't how this progressively earlier start date happened, but it's my theory that decades of no daylight saving time in Indiana have thrown our whole summer out of whack and nobody knows when the school year is supposed to start anymore.

The scientists who think we are experiencing global warming should consider the school calendar. It could be that just by making the first day of school in August instead of September, we're making the world seem much hotter than it is.

There are too many reminders of how short the summer vacation is. My son got out of school on June 2, and on June 17 there were back-to-school sales at Staples and Kohl's. I would have taken advantage of those opportunities, but they were having a winter coat special at Burlington and I didn't want to miss out.

I'm no expert, but if I remember my school history (as in, the history of schools), the whole point of summer vacation was so that kids could help out on the farm. If in 1894 they had started school during the state fair, you'd have had a lot of fathers bent out of shape and more than a few heifers in a snit. No self-respecting Hoosier farmer was going to drag a three-hundred-pound pig to the fair while his son or daughter was lounging around a classroom having fun diagramming sentences and doing multiplication tables.

I can tell you this. If I had a cow that I wanted to show at the fair and my son was at Lawrence North High School, I'd write this note for him to give to his principal.

Dear Ms. Lupold:

Brett will not be in school today. He has a sore throat and an upset stomach that will last from Tuesday, August 17, until Sunday, August 22. He is willing to make up the work. You can drop off his zoology assignments at the elephant ear concession and his physics homework at the Ferris wheel.

When I was kid back in New York, school did not begin until after Labor Day. When there was talk of beginning school a week or so earlier in August, a strike was threatened. Not just by the students—by the teachers, too. My best friend, Eric, stood up at a PTA meeting and made a case for a post-Labor Day start by analyzing the appropriate number of school days based on the heat index and factoring in the emotional trauma of beginning school too early. Eric was from a very wealthy family so his argument lost some ground when he advocated the right to summer in Paris during all of August. "August is a summer month," he said steely-eyed to the association's board president. "You could look it up."

We all got a kick out of this. Eric was a great debater, but a lousy student. He had to go to summer school every year. As a result, his summer vacation (the time between the end of summer school and regular school) was down to about forty-eight hours. Eric was trying to squeeze in a swim before he had to start Algebra II for the third time.

My son will begin college soon. At one school we have looked into, the academic year ends April 17 and does not begin again until September 25. I don't know what Brett will do with such a long summer vacation. I hope he comes home.

I think he'd get a kick out of the state fair.

Wake-Up Hauls

Are you busy Saturday or Sunday mornings between five and seven o'clock?

I need someone to play with.

Trust me, this is not a naughty proposition. I'm just so bored I can barely stand it.

You see, during the week, I get up at 3:30 A.M. in order to do my show on Channel 8. When the weekend rolls around, I can't shift my body clock. At 4:30 I'm ready to go outside, throw my arms around the morning, grab the day by the lapels, and embrace the rising sun.

On Saturday mornings, my wife and son sleep until about, oh, let's say Sunday. By 5 A.M., I've painted the garage, walked the dog, and waxed the car. I'm still bored so I wax the garage, paint the car, and vacuum the dog.

Finally, I can't stand it anymore so long about 6 A.M. I get in the car to run a few errands. But the retail world just doesn't want to cooperate.

My first stop is the bank. Incredibly, the bank does not open until nine o'clock. ON MONDAY. What are these people thinking? What is a guy like me supposed to do at 6 A.M. ON SUNDAY when he needs two fives for a ten? Do you think America will ever bounce back from its financial ruin? I don't think so. Not when at sunrise on a Sunday, all thirty-seven thousand tellers in America are still asleep.

Off to the dry cleaner. I read the sign: NOW WE ARE OPEN SUNDAYS AT NOON. Like I'm impressed. I've got my tuxedo crumpled up in a bag and a formal event on my social calendar only three months away. Maybe you like cutting things close, but not me. Show me a dry cleaning store that opens at six o'clock Saturday morning, and I'll show you a company that is headed for the Fortune 500. Hey, it's a dirty job, but someone has to do it.

I try the barbershop. Closed. Does hair stop growing until the sun rises? Am I the only person in America who wants a good haircut at 6 A.M.? Hey, I heard what you said under your breath. You chuckled to yourself and said, "How about werewolves?" Who's writing this humor column, anyway?

What about the post office? Nope. Another stupid government decision. The U.S. post office doesn't open until eight o'clock on Saturday. Have these people never heard of market research? You can't tell me they wouldn't sell a truckload of stamps between 6 and 8 A.M. That's lost revenues. Forever. You don't have to go to the Wharton School of Business to know that.

One last try. Lowe's: not open. Menards: doors locked. Home Depot: a ghost town. Staples: forget it. Office Depot: CLOSED.

Now it's almost 7 A.M. I pull into the Shell station. Yes, the gas station is open. But I don't need gas. I could use a car wash, but the car wash doesn't open until 8, which is kinda nuts since the whole thing is completely automatic to begin with.

I'm so desperate by this point that I'm thinking of going to the Super Wal-Mart. Wal-Mart is open. It never closes. But the optical department doesn't open until 9 A.M. And there is no one in electronics until nine either. Same with the photo shop. And the snack bar. The sign should read: WE ARE PARTIALLY OPEN TWENTY-FOUR HOURS A DAY.

And now I'm getting very, very frustrated. And angry. This is not an appropriate response. I know I need some counseling—some therapy to deal with this problem. But help is hard to find.

Especially on a Saturday morning at 6 A.M.

Black Holes

There was a point last week when I realized I was missing the following items:

1. My garage door opener
2. My keys
3. My reading glasses
4. My pillow

This is the most that's ever gotten lost. Wait, that sounds odd. Maybe I should say: This is the most that I have ever had lost. That doesn't sound right, either. One thing is sure: This is the most lost I've ever been. There, that's it.

Anyway, I usually put a list on my bulletin board of the things in my life that are presently missing. Then I check each one off as I find it. This gives me a feeling of accomplishment. I admit I am one of the world's great losers, but at least I am aware of who I am. Once I admitted to myself what a loser I was, I knew I had found myself—one of the few things, by the way, not lost at 10:43 P.M. on Wednesday night.

I have written about losing things before, but this time I want to take you through my personal journey on how to find things in the hopes that it may assist you in finding yourself, or whatever it is that you have lost.

My Garage Door Opener: I knew that I was in the house and that there is no way to get in my house from the car without coming through the garage. And I would have no reason to take the garage door opener from my car. Ergo (whatever that means), the garage door opener is still in the car. This gave me such a feeling of elation that I raced out to the garage, threw open the doors to my car, and scoured every inch of the vehicle. I never found it. So, now when I drive home, I have to get out of the car, go around to the side door of the garage, go inside and hit the switch, then get back in the car, drive into the garage, and close the door manually. This may seem like a small inconvenience, but it pales in comparison to the euphoria I feel knowing the opener is not lost after all. It's in the car. I crossed it off my list.

My Keys: I looked for my car keys for two hours. Nothing. Nowhere. I then applied a similar logic to that of the garage door opener. I observed that I was home. I further noted that just yesterday I was somewhere else.

Then I did that ergo thing again and realized that the only way to get from where I was to where I am was by traveling. Once again a great weight was lifted (I wish it were the garage door) as I realized that my car keys were somewhere in my house. I have repeated this story to several of my cab drivers over the past week, and they all find it mildly amusing as well as extremely profitable. One driver says he has a dozen customers who haven't lost their keys, just like me. I crossed keys off my list.

My Reading Glasses: Once again, I applied inescapable logic to my dilemma. I can't read a lick without my reading glasses, yet as I examined my psyche I realized that at 10:43 P.M. on a Wednesday night, I knew that the TV critic for the *Indianapolis Star* had written a favorable review of a dinosaur special on the Discovery Channel. How could I know that unless I had read it? How could I have read it unless I was wearing my glasses? Ergo again. My glasses were not lost at all; they were somewhere in the house. If only I could see, I would be able to find them. Three down, one to go.

My Pillow: I applied the very same logic to my missing pillow. This time, however, I am sad to report that my pillow is, in fact, really lost.

So much for logic.

Better Read This

This month marks my twenty-fifth year in television.

It seems like just yesterday I was nervously standing in front of a camera, not sure which direction to look, unprepared for my segment, babbling away incoherently.

Wait a second; that was yesterday.

This insight has made me realize there are countless things in my life that I am no better at now than I was when I started on this earth fifty-six years ago. Here are the top ten things I am not any better at. You might ask yourself the same questions.

1. Am I a better dresser? For fifty-plus years, I've been getting up in the morning and trying to match a shirt with a pair of pants. I still ask my wife before we go out, "Does this look okay?"

For twenty-five years she's responded the same way: "Don't you have any gray pants?"

2. Am I a better driver? Forty years of driving, and I still have half the world honking at me to get in my own lane. People still flip me the bird and shake their fist at me, just like when I was sixteen. Forty years—no improvement. Don't feel sorry for me. Just get out of my way.

3. Am I a better golfer? Not by a single stroke. In fact, I'm worse. My handicap in college was ten, now it's eleven. Two thousand rounds of golf, 4,000 golf balls, 160,000 swings, 10,000 expletives...and not a lick better. I'm depressed just writing about this. But not enough to cancel my tee time.

4. Do I have a better sense of direction? When I was a toddler, I got lost in my own house, a two-bedroom ranch. Fifty years later, I can go to the same office building one thousand times and I still don't know which way to turn when I get out of the elevator. When I was forty years old, I finally realized that north was up on a map. That doesn't work when you are driving.

5. Am I a better judge of character? I asked

some of my new friends this and they said I was definitely improving. Hmmm...

6. Am I a better dancer? I have been dancing for forty-five years. I do that gyrating thing where you snap your fingers and every once in a while you turn around. I will tell you honestly that I still can't do that to the music. I know I look ridiculous and the only reason people don't laugh is they are doing the very same thing, fortunately looking at their own feet.

7. Am I better at fixing things? I thought I was, but my handyman Steve charges me thirty dollars an hour to repair things around my house unless I try to help him. Then it starts to get really expensive.

8. Am I a better father? I asked my son. His reply: "Do you mean better than Eric's father?" I decided to drop it.

9. (This one is none of your business.)

10. Am I a better writer? Not based on this essay. But I'll keep trying.

You know what they say: Practice makes perfect.

Anger Management

Once a year I write a column about all the things that annoy me. This is an important exercise for me because most of the time I write about things that make me laugh—but then all the annoying stuff builds up inside me and I need some way to release it.

I believe in letting the little things bother me. I can't do anything about the big things, so I let tiny, inconsequential things drive me nuts with the idea that I might be able to change them. Here are a few examples:

Restaurant Buzzer:

What idiot thought of this idea? Before the buzzer, people would lounge around the waiting area and every five minutes they would walk up to the front and say, "Excuse me, but how long 'til my table is ready?" Now, through the miracles of technology, people lounge around the waiting area and every five minutes walk up and ask, "How long 'til my buzzer goes off?"

Valet Parking:

My fitness center has valet parking for people who don't want to walk from their car to the front door of a facility where they are going to climb a Stairmaster for two hours. Do I need to say anything more about this?

Cell Phone Messages:

When I call some of my friends on their cell phones, the message says, "I can't get to the phone right now." What do you mean, you can't get to the phone? The phone is in your pocket, Kevin. Answer it!

Department Extensions:

I called a company in Hammond, Indiana, the other day. The extension of the woman I was directed to was 74123. But there are only four people in her entire office. Who invented this concept? It's the same guy who made my house 8210. Where are the other 8200 houses on my block?

Homework:

I think teachers give too much homework on weekends. My son spent every Saturday last year doing homework. When I was a teacher, I never gave homework on the weekends. Come to think of it, I seldom gave homework. The kids loved me, the parents loved me, and I had nothing to grade when I got home. You'd think this concept would have caught on.

"Will That Be All, Sir?"

I'm pretty sure Andy Rooney has done this one. It drives me crazy when the cashier scans my candy bar and says, "Will that be all?"

"No, I forgot the washer-dryer and the Brussels sprouts. Thanks for reminding me."

Discount Cards:

I refuse to carry a Marsh, Kroger, CVS, Panera, Walgreens, Blockbuster, Einstein Bagels, Staples, Office Depot, Menards, Lowe's, or any other card for a discount. Read my lips. I AM IN YOUR STORE. I AM BUYING SOMETHING FROM YOU. DO YOU NEED ANY OTHER PROOF THAT I AM A GOOD CUSTOMER? THANK YOU FOR TAKING DICK WOLFSIE'S MONEY. Now they have a Hallmark Card card. Stop me before I choke the clerk.

$1.50 for Coffee:

And finally, I don't want to pay to make my own coffee in a hotel room. Last week I was in Columbus, Ohio, at a very nice hotel. It was $175 a night. They charged me $1.50 to make my own coffee in the room. Would they charge me $1.50 to make my own bed? Make the room $176.50 and give me free coffee!

Well, that's it for now. If some of this stuff does not make you angry, you'll probably find yourself in my column next year. People like you annoy me, too.

Thought for Food

Just when you thought it was safe to enjoy lunch, the U.S. Government has come out with new guidelines for good eating. "Good" is clearly the wrong word here, because it is only good in their eyes. But in our mouths, everything they're pushing tastes an awful lot like broccoli. And I say the heck with it.

Years ago, the percentages of each type of food the government recommended were represented in a pie chart. This was a bad idea because as soon as people saw that image, they got a craving for a big slice of apple or cherry.

Then they introduced a pyramid to portray the correct amounts of food from each food category. I like the pyramid image because it makes me think of the incredible toil that went into building one of those structures in ancient Egypt, and I find that more effective than salted nuts in motivating me to drink beer.

The newest illustration has some skinny guy running up one side of the pyramid. Within the triangle are bands of color, each depicting a different food group. Blue, for example, represents dairy. This is confusing because anyone who knows anything (or has listened to a George Carlin monologue) knows there is no such thing as blue food.

Then we learn that the wider the band in the pyramid, the more of that food we should eat. This has really thrown me, because my whole life I have believed that the wider the band is around your own structure, the less of that food you should eat.

Last time the research was published, the government recommended eleven servings of vegetables a day. This seemed excessive to the average person (who also needed to drink nine glasses of water daily), so the government has changed the recommendation from eleven servings to three cups of vegetables. But if you read the fine print, three cups is equal to eleven servings. These are the same people who are balancing our budget and telling us that even though our national deficit is a gazillion dollars, it is only 2 percent of our gross national product, so it's okay, don't worry about it. Ain't numbers fun?

And there was still more big news. "Big" is the

operative word here. According to the paper, the government now says that being overweight doesn't carry the death risk they originally thought. They said they got the math wrong. How could that be? I balance my bank statement with a six-dollar calculator from Staples and I've never been more than a penny off. Now here comes the U.S. Government trying to deal with life and death statistics, and they say, "We miscalculated." You know, for another three bucks you can get the calculator with the really BIG numbers. That's just a suggestion from a concerned citizen.

Then the article says that being "moderately overweight" is actually a good thing. People who tip the scales four to six pounds more than was previously thought to be ideal actually live longer. I'm no Harvard nutritionist, but it seems to me that they have this a little mixed up. You don't live longer because you are overweight; it's just that the government's definition of overweight was wrong. By the way, that last line was *not* supposed to be funny. Sometimes I fear that in a humor column, people just brush off brilliant insights. That was one of them.

The article goes on to say that being overweight leads to fewer deaths than car accidents. The old statistics were muddled because researchers did not know what to do with people who were killed in their cars while eating a triple-dip Ben and Jerry's ice cream cone.

This obsession with weight has always caused some tension between my chubby friends and me. They used to say that because I could eat anything I wanted and still maintain my trim waist size, it was just killing them.

Now, apparently, it's killing me.

Price Hypes

I just discovered that there is a Web site for cheap-skates called Cheapskate.com. It's advice and tips for penny-pinching skinflints who will do anything to save a buck. There's also a book for people who are cheap, but it sells for $29.95 so I don't see this making the bestseller list. Of course, I didn't think the book *Learn to Read* would ever take off either, so don't go by me.

I do think a Web site for cheap people is a good idea. In fact, I'd even like to start my own, but I understand there may be some cost involved, so I'm already having second thoughts.

When I was a kid, my mom said I was cheap. She figured out that every year on Mother's Day I recycled the previous year's card so I wouldn't have to buy her a new one. I'm not sure where I got this cheapness quality. By the way, Mom caught my father doing the same thing for her birthday.

Growing up, I bought lots of stuff at a place called the Five and Dime. Now I buy lots of stuff at the dollar store. I'm beating myself up over the fact I didn't stock up while I had the chance. Who knew?

In high school, I'd hear guys talking about some girl who had a reputation for being cheap. I assumed that meant she wouldn't split the cost of the movie. So I never asked those girls out. Then I found out what it really meant and I could have kicked myself.

Sometimes you hear the expression "a cheap shot" or "a cheap trick." Why are people paying anything for shots and tricks? I think with a little cajoling, you can get shots and tricks for free. I'd put that on my Web site.

And they say talk is cheap. Which is why these essays are printed. I'd call you on the phone and read them to you, but I just don't see you coughing up the big bucks. Say, who's the cheap one now?

"Cheaper by the dozen" is another expression you often hear. I thought that seemed very unlikely, and sure enough I got laughed out of a Krispy Kreme Donut Shop when I insisted on paying less for a dozen donuts than for one. And what about "Two can live as cheaply as one"? That notion catapulted me right into marriage when I was only thirty-five. Since Mary Ellen had a good job, I think we did manage to live as inexpensively as when I was single...if you don't count her pedicures.

My wife thinks I'm cheap because I don't want to go into an expensive restaurant with her and blow a hundred dollars for dinner. If I believed in tipping, it would be even more expensive.

I don't think I'm cheap. I don't turn out lights in a room when I exit; I leave the front door open in the dead of winter, and I throw out leftovers instead of putting them in Tupperware. I also won't take the time to drive the additional block where I know gas is a dime a gallon less expensive. My wife says this does not mean I am not cheap. It means I am stupid. Say, who asked you to nod your head?

Of course, I think my wife is cheap. She cuts out coupons and shops during sales. She says that is being frugal, not cheap. Say, what is it with the head nodding?

That's about all I have to say about being cheap. Next time you see me, I may be behind you when you pull out of your parking space. That is, if you've left fifteen minutes on the meter.

Seals of Disapproval

I don't have a lot of friends. Oh, I know lots of people, but that's not the same.

A friend will sleep at your house for two weeks while you're skiing in Vail so your plants won't die. Someone you "know" won't do that.

A friend will take your children to a rock concert because you have tickets to the Pacers the same night. Someone you "know" won't do that.

A friend will shovel your driveway after a huge storm just because. Someone you "know" won't do that.

Admit it. You don't have any friends either, do you?

Not having a lot of friends has its advantages. My wife never says, "Gosh, Dick, we haven't gone out with the Goldbergs in two weeks. I hope they're not angry at us." Or, "You know, Dick, we need to have a dinner party to pay back the Fabershams for their St. Patrick's Day gala."

Actually, the Wolfsies seldom attend galas. But the other day, I did learn the hard way the negative results of our limited social menu.

Mary Ellen and I attended a party called Zoo Fest. I think a fest is kinda like a gala, but I don't have enough experience to make a sweeping statement like that. Part of the Fest was a silent auction to raise money for the zoo. A silent auction is where people lurk around a huge table trying to purchase a year's supply of oil changes for twenty bucks.

I'm not very successful at these events and it always puts me in a rotten mood when I discover that my five dollar bid for an eight-hour limo ride for ten is always a few dollars short. Personally, I have found it more profitable to hang around the buffet table and suck up shrimp at twenty-two bucks a pound.

I do, however, always make an opening bid on items hoping that my celebrity status will get the ball rolling. So at Zoo Fest, when I bid a measly one hundred bucks for the right to feed the seals, I figured that I would create a juggernaut of interest.

Two days later, this came in the mail:

> **CONGRATULATIONS, YOU'VE WON!**
>
> *Feed the seals at the Indianapolis Zoo*
>
> Four people
>
> (expires Sept 30, 2004)

Reality set in. I had five weeks to find three people who would want to feed the seals with me.

"Hi Rob, it's Dick Wolfsie. Say, I'm trying to get a group of people together to feed some seals."

"Gee Dick, only you, in landlocked Indiana, could find homeless, hungry seals."

"You don't understand, these are not homeless, hungry seals. These are well-fed, happy seals."

"Then you need to find a more deserving charity, Dick. Cast out your philanthropic net. Aren't we saving whales anymore? Or bald eagles?"

"You don't understand. I bought this at Zoo Fest for a hundred dollars."

"Yeah, I was there, too. I got the limo ride for ten people for forty bucks. I don't seem to be having any problems finding friends."

I tried Mikki. She loves animals....

"Mikki, how would you like to feed some seals with me?"

"Dick, I'm no animal nutritionist, but I get the feeling that this request requires holding dead fish."

"Yes, I think it does."

CLICK.

I think that next time I'll bid on the condo in Vail for six people. I'll have better luck finding friends for that one. But I'll probably end up staying at home.

Someone has to water the plants.

Pig Tales

I know you have heard of bad hair days and bad work days. And of course, there are always bad weather days. But last Tuesday I had a bad food day. And it wasn't the things I ate. It was the things I didn't eat.

It all started with a TV segment on how to barbecue a pork roast by injecting it with a hypodermic needle filled with marinade. Just the idea of this was enough to make my tongue do the cha cha. When the chef gave me a pre-injected piece of meat to grill at home, I knew my Weber grill was about to perform a culinary miracle.

Then I made a fatal mistake. I put the roast in the company refrigerator and forgot it was there. This is the equivalent of leaving your PalmPilot on a bench at Grand Central Station in New York City.

The next day, it was gone. In its place were two

cold slices of Domino's pizza and a loaf of no-carb bread. Yuck.

I do not think anyone stole my dinner. I think it was taken by someone who meant to take home their week-old portion of moo shu pork that was in a white Styrofoam container and by accident grabbed an eight-pound uncooked pork roast that was double-wrapped in aluminum foil. Mistakes happen.

I myself have never taken anyone's lunch, but will admit to pulling a few slices of corned beef out of a Shapiro's deli sandwich in that very fridge, a technique I perfected as a babysitter some forty years ago. You then fold the remaining meat over so that to an untrained eye…wait a second, did you think I was going to tell you all my secrets?

I went home that afternoon very depressed, but I rejoiced when I realized that in my refrigerator at home was a succulent barbeque chicken breast that I had prepared the night before on a slow charcoal flame after it had marinated overnight.

I raced into the kitchen and swung open the refrigerator door.

The pork purloiner was now a poultry poacher.

But wait, this was not the modus operandi of a roast thief. They tend to work in the business setting, seldom straying to suburban neighborhoods. There was only one explanation for this despicable act: My wife took my chicken breast.

Imagine that! My wife, guilty of lunch larceny. I was sure that there was some cruel penalty for this shameful act clearly proscribed in the Talmud or the Old Testament—some horrific punishment for coveting your husband's chicken breast enough to take it to work. I didn't recall that the retribution was as severe as it was for adultery, but it had to be appropriately close.

I called Mary Ellen at work. "What are you doing, Dear?"

"Sitting here at my desk having a delicious lunch I brought from home."

"I see. And when you took that delicious lunch out of the fridge this morning, did you give any moral consideration to whom that breast originally belonged?"

"To a chicken, I assume. Oh dear. Are you going through your animal rights phase again?"

During our brief discussion I was reminded that the house was ours, the refrigerator was ours, the teenager was ours, and the dog was ours. But apparently, the night after a family barbecue, the leftover chicken breast is hers.

And I thought I didn't need a prenuptial agreement.

Movie Madness

I'm not boasting, but I have always thought of myself as an intelligent person.

I've got a degree from a pretty good school. I read several books a month. The people from Mensa tell me that if I hadn't gotten lost on the way to the qualification exam, I might have gotten into their organization of brainy people.

But I have my limitations. Maps, for example, remain a mystery to me. Sometimes when I'm heading to a TV remote shoot, people will say, "Just go to MapQuest on your computer." MapQuest is a Web site that tells you how to get across your street by making only twelve turns. I can't read a MapQuest map. I can't download a MapQuest map. And even if I could print it, how the heck do you read a map that doesn't have twelve folds in it?

But my real limitation is movies. I never understand them. Ever. When I go to the movies with my family, I sit between my teenage son and my wife so that I can turn in either direction for an explanation. During *Harry Potter* I asked my son so many questions that he moved to another seat next to a seven-year-old who apparently understood everything. (It helps if you have read the book first.)

I drive my wife crazy, also. She claims that if I paid better attention, I wouldn't ask so many stupid questions.

"Why are people jumping off that ship, Mary Ellen?"

"It's the Titanic, Dick. Is all the screaming interrupting your nap?"

"Mary Ellen, why did that man just jump out of the plane?"

"Dick, I don't know. No one knows. This is called a preview."

"Mary Ellen, why did that woman just stab that guy?"

"Well, he killed her husband, stole her money, and burned her house down. Those are the only clues the viewer has been given."

I can't be the only one who feels this way. I think part of the problem is that filmmakers look for ways to perplex the viewer, thinking that makes the movie more artsy. I believe that movie creators should spend some time in the slammer if they do any of the following:

Flashbacks: If there is going to a flashback in a movie, there should be a big sign in the theater next to the screen that says, FLASHBACKS AT 7:37 P.M. and 8:42 P.M. Sometimes I sit through a whole movie confused, until my wife says, "Dick, you are confused because what you are watching happened twenty-five years ago. It's called a FLASHBACK." Which is a reminder to me that I want my MONEYBACK.

Dream Sequence: This is when the character either dreams or imagines everything on the screen. In the old TV sitcoms, when a person was having a dream you got this campy music and the picture kind of swirled and dissolved to show the person had fallen asleep. Gee, I guess special effects are hard to do nowadays.

Prequels and Sequels: While watching *Star Wars*, my son informed me that I probably didn't understand everything because they made the second episode first. "On purpose?" I asked him. You'd think with five hundred people on the production set, someone would say, "I think we forgot to do Part I."

Reverse Order: Every once in a while, a filmmaker makes a movie where the story starts at the end and then goes to the beginning. Except for this one example of human misjudgment, I am generally opposed to capital punishment.

I'll still go to the movies. I'll pay my dollar to get in. Then twenty-five cents for a bag of popcorn and ten cents for a Coke.

By the way, that was a flashback. You were confused for a second, weren't you?

Life-Changing Experience

I got a letter in the mail the other day that was pretty special, and I'd like to share it with you.

Dear Dick,

Thank you so very much for your sensitivity, generosity, and kindness. You will never know what a difference you made in my life.

Jerry

I just had one question. Who's Jerry?
Mary Ellen thought I was making this up.

"How can you not know who Jerry is? You changed his life."

"I know, I know, but the name doesn't ring a bell."

"Fine, but doesn't the changing his life part ring a bell?"

This was very frustrating for me because I'm not really that wonderful a guy and I usually don't do a great deal of life changing. In fact, I'd say I change someone's life only about once every six or eight years so you'd think I'd remember a guy named Jerry. Nope. Not a clue.

I went back through my appointment book to see if I had made any appointments that had life-altering possibilities.

It was actually kind of depressing because I saw no potential in the last six months for any such accomplishment. In fact, I didn't have much evidence in my appointment calendar for any displays of sensitivity or generosity. Truth is, if I had gotten a letter from someone saying:

Dear Dick:

You insensitive, ungenerous lout. You are not a very kind person. Thanks for messing up my life.

Well, a letter like that I could understand. Wouldn't even need my appointment book.

But this one? Jerry? Jerry? Wait a second, maybe it wasn't Jerry at all. Maybe it was his wife, or his son, or his daughter whose life I changed and that's why I couldn't place the name. Of course! And all this time I had been berating myself for not remembering *Jerry's* name. I'm glad that's over. Now it won't bother me.

God help me. Who is Jerry?

Wait, I had an idea. I went to my computer and typed in "Jerry." Now we were getting somewhere. There were two million Web sites with the name Jerry—the first 200 had something to do with gourmet ice cream, the next 300 were fan clubs for *Leave It to Beaver*, and 250 more for Jerry Springer.

I don't like Ben and Jerry's Ice Cream. When I eat it, my head freezes up and I get a terrible headache, but I don't think that's the kind of sensitivity Jerry meant.

I started to wonder if I had ever affected Jerry Mathers's life. I interviewed him once on my TV show and told him how much I loved the show where he got caught in the coffee cup on the billboard. I also told him that Eddie Haskell was a jerk and a slime, so I don't think I earned the sensitivity label. Nah. Not Jerry Mathers.

And Jerry Springer? Wow, I've met him also. But I don't think he even knows the words "kind" and "sensitive."

I tried to narrow the search on the computer: Jerry/Dick/Generous/Sensitive. Nothing. Not one example came up. Well, there was my answer. Jerry may have thought I changed his life, but I didn't. That's why I couldn't remember. It was some random act of kindness that I bestowed on someone—someone whose name I never got.

I started feeling better about myself. I had helped someone and asked for nothing in return. Not even the person's name. I am a kind and generous guy. I have changed a life and I had no motive other than the knowledge that I made a difference. I was content.

Please God, who is Jerry?

Part 2

Sheepish Grins
(More RAMblings about Life)

Fishy Story

This has been a bad week for people like me who get their medical news from the newspaper. Especially since I read the paper over my first cup of coffee.

It was confusing enough that coffee was first thought to be bad for you, then good for you. Then they were sure it caused heart attacks, but it prevented strokes—except for decaf, which not only caused strokes, but was related to diabetes.

I'm sure I got that all wrong, but so what? The paper comes out again tomorrow.

I was so confused a few years ago about whether or not peanuts were good for me that it actually drove me to start drinking. That was a good thing because they said alcohol helped your heart, but it ended up being a bad thing because then they said it wasn't the alcohol that was beneficial, but the grapes. And I had been drinking beer. That ended up being a good thing because then they announced the hops were good for you but the carbs were bad, so now I'm going to CA meetings (Carbs Anonymous).

Well, as I said, this week took the cake. Cake, by the way, is not good for you, unless it's chocolate, which has some kind of aphrodisiac in it. But it also has caffeine, which is bad for you (unless it's the same amount of caffeine that was good for you if you were drinking coffee June through August of 2004).

This week I learned that salmon is not good for you. Ever since the first report that salmon had omega fatty acids several years ago, I've been chowing down on anything that swims upstream to die: coho, chinook, king, pink and sockeye. I have eaten it smoked, pickled, fresh, and canned. If my heart wasn't bright red before, it is now.

Yes, I wanted those omega fatty acids. I had no idea what they were. But I knew where to get them.

Then I saw this headline:

FARMED SALMON MORE DANGEROUS TO EAT THAN WILD SALMON

At first, I thought they got it mixed up. Those wild salmon lead quite a life. I figure if you're willing to die just for a couple of weeks of casual spawning, you're probably willing to eat anything that swims by.

Of course, statistics about danger can be misleading. Maybe some of those people fishing for wild salmon were eaten by bears. That's the kind of data that gets lost in those fancy university studies.

But no, farmed salmon is apparently worse. At least today. So I decided to adjust my diet accordingly. In the supermarket it's hard to tell wild from farm-raised. They all look pretty dead to me, making it difficult to see any wanderlust in their eyes.

I asked for the manager of the supermarket.

"See this salmon, here? Where was it born?"

"I don't know, sir. It's hard to tell when it's in a can."

I'm not sure what I'm going to do next. I love salmon. In fact, I have three salmon patties in my fridge right now, waiting to be sautéed in a pan with a little butter.

It's four in the morning as I write this essay. The newspaper should be here any minute and I can check to see what I'm supposed to eat. In the meantime, I'll have a cup of coffee and a couple of peanuts. See you next week.

If I live that long.

Good Morning?

I can't wait to get up in the morning and go to work. And the older I get the more I feel that way. People think it is because I have a wonderful job, love my co-workers, and have a great boss. No, those are not the reasons. Trust me.

The real reason is I am trying desperately to avoid my family.

Recently, I was given very specific directives from my wife and son. I am not to talk to them in the morning on certain days of the week: Sunday, Thursday, Tuesday, Monday, Saturday, Friday, and Wednesday.

It is now the consensus in my house that I am in too good a mood in the morning and it is apparently getting on everyone's nerves.

When Brett and Mary Ellen awaken, this is apparently the worst they feel all day. This troubles me because I have heard heavy drinkers make the very same claim about mornings.

I have always been a morning person. In college, I would awaken at 4 A.M. and begin to study. My roommate had no problem with this, until he walked in the door at 4:30 A.M. from a date and he asked me to turn off the light.

"Why are you so darn happy when you wake up?" asked my wife. "You even whistle before you go to work. Do you know how annoying that is? Only you would do that."

"Not so, Mary Ellen. I can name several people who do that."

"Go ahead."

"Grumpy, Sneezy, Doc, Happy…"

"Hey, no fair counting family."

My wife has developed a few phrases to remind me she wants nothing to do with me in the morning.

"What's so good about it?"

"Don't talk to me until I've had my lunch."

"If you try to say one more funny thing, I'll rip your face off."

"You want to do *what* in the morning? You must be thinking it's still our honeymoon. Look, Dick, I sleep on my face all night. My hair looks like Don King's. I haven't brushed my teeth in half a day and I can't see because my contact lenses aren't in. What do you say to that?"

"Wow, when you put it that way, I'm glad the honeymoon is over."

The other morning, I tried to relate to what my wife was saying. I got up at the crack of dawn and looked in the mirror. I usually don't pay that much attention, but I realized that at 5:00 A.M., my face was mostly a nose and a large forehead. I think I saw one or two ears.

But I was still in a good mood. I told my wife that although I'm a morning person, I could be as pleasant and good-natured at 9 P.M. as I am at 9 A.M. Of course, I wouldn't want her to put me to the test. I hate being awakened in the middle of the night.

Knows Cone

Let us all celebrate the one hundredth anniversary of the ice cream cone. Wait—not so fast! Like other great inventions in history, there is some controversy about when the first cone was really created...and who did the creating. Some say it was Italo Marchiony, others say Charles Menches, and who could forget Antonio Valvano? Apparently, everybody.

It's the same with the sandwich. Some people think it was the Earl of Sandwich back in the late 1700s. No one has confirmed this, but the name says it all. I went to school with a Herb Cohn, but his family came to New York in the 1890s and made a killing in the garment industry, so it wasn't Herb's family that invented the cone, I can tell you that.

Remember that the telephone, television, airplane, and electric light bulb were not discovered in a flash, but were ideas nurtured by a number of people over many years. Sometimes the person who got the credit was the best businessman or the one who lived closest to the patent office.

But what about that ice cream cone? One theorist contends it was invented even before ice cream by some forward-thinking genius who knew he had a good idea, but soon realized that most people just weren't in the market for an edible pastry to hold rocks and small insects.

So while credit for the invention of the ice cream cone remains a swirling controversy, I maintain the biggest mystery is why it ever caught on in the first place.

An ice cream cone is poorly designed. Because of the pointed bottom, you can't set it down. There is one kind of cone that has a flat bottom; it also has no taste. I once asked an ice cream executive why they didn't make the sugar cones with a flat bottom. TRADITION, he bellowed. Hey, I want to put my cone down so I can make a left-hand turn while I'm on my cell phone. The heck with tradition.

The ice cream cone is also poorly constructed. Half the time it crumbles when you try to force the ice cream scoop on top. If the ice cream is soft and you pack it down, by the time you've taken the tenth lick, it's leaking out the bottom, all over your new beige corduroy pants.

A lot of times, if you're a strong licker, the whole round scoop falls off in a big plop. And there's no five-second rule for ice cream. When it hits the ground, it's history.

Imagine if the cup had been invented after the cone. Here are the headlines:

CONES ARE OUT, CUPS INVENTED
- No more dripping
- No crumbling
- Give your tongue a rest

"But wait," you say, "you can't eat a dish." That's true. So we should just be thankful we have two alternatives for America's favorite frozen food. What would it be like if people had to carry around a scoop of ice cream in their bare hands?

I shudder to think.

Fast Cash

Over the past year, I have been giving the fast food people kind of a hard time. Making fun of these folks is very un-American of me and I am going to stop it right now. After all, statistics show that twenty million people order fast food every day. They don't actually get what they order, but they do order it. Darn, there I go again.

Now, according to an article in the paper a few weeks back, Janice Meissner, a mother of three, ordered a bagel and a regular Coke at McDonald's. This is the only recorded case of a mother of three ordering just a Coke and a bagel. This really confused her kids because they were on the Atkins diet. But that's not what this story is about.

When she opened the bag, instead of a bagel, she found three thousand in cash. I am not making this up.

Talk about a Happy Meal!

The McDonald's people say the money had been placed in a take-out sack for security reasons so no one would steal it.

Then, apparently, the bag was placed too close to the window and then given to Ms. Meissner by mistake. Do they teach this stuff at McDonald's Hamburger College? Okay, this is none of my business, but HOW ABOUT A SAFE? They keep hamburger patties worth about six cents each in huge metal refrigerators that require a combination to get into. And employees have to sign a non-compete clause just to handle that special sauce. Then they put three grand in a paper bag and put it by the drive-up window. HELLLOOOO?

When Ms. Meissner opened the bag, she was not happy....

"That is the third time this week you screwed up my order," she complained. "Can't you people get anything right?" she yelled through the intercom.

"Sorry, Madam. What did we give you?"

"Looks like mostly twenty dollar bills and lots of tens and fives."

"Did you want fries with that?"

"NO, I don't want fries with that. I wanted a Coke and a bagel. Is that so difficult?"

"Could you pull up front? We'll have to make it special for you."

"What about the money?"

"No charge, it was our mistake."

"No! I mean what's in the bag, now. Don't you want it back?"

"Oh, the Board of Health won't permit us to resell an order. Just enjoy."

"Let me explain this one more time. There is green stuff in this bag. Lots of green stuff. I don't want GREEN STUFF."

"Okay, okay. Ordering a Coke and a bagel. HOLD THE LETTUCE."

"Let me try this one more time. In this bag is cold, hard cash. How could that happen?"

"We think it's the microwave oven. We've been having a problem all week."

Ms. Meissner finally called McDonald's and returned the money.

When all this was straightened out, Ms. Meissner received a letter in the mail. When she opened it up, she found a fifty-dollar gift certificate for Burger King.

"I just enjoyed my ten Whoppers," said the mother of three. "Heaven knows, I wasn't going to say anything."

Fat Chance of Success!

A couple of fast food restaurants have come out with a new product to appeal to those misguided people who now, after years of giving up meat, have decided to eschew the bun and start chewing the fat.

We all knew that if we waited long enough, something that was bad for us would end up being good for us. We just didn't know if we'd live long enough to find out. But I'd chow down real quick. According to my resources, carbs will be back in favor by Super Bowl XL. And by Super Bowl L, instead of steak on a stick, people will be eating just the sticks. Talk about a fiber craze.

The new trend has resulted in a new menu choice: a hamburger with pickles, onion, lettuce, tomato, ketchup, mustard, and mayonnaise, but no bun.

A lot of you are saying: Wait a second! How can you

eat a hamburger with pickles, onion, lettuce, tomato, ketchup, mustard, and mayonnaise—but no bun?

This very question came up at a corporate meeting when the Hardee's marketing department endorsed the concept. These were the same people who advocated the Six-Dollar Burger for four dollars. Which required a HUGE bun.

These people would have been fired, but federal regulations make it illegal to fire someone just because of the size of their buns.

It was Harvey, the great-grandson of the founder of Hardee's, who while working at corporate headquarters during his summer break first said, "Excuse me, I know I'm just a college kid with no common sense and heir to the Hardee's fortune, but how do you eat a hamburger with pickles, onion, lettuce, tomato, ketchup, mustard, and mayonnaise, but no bun? When people come to the drive-up window and want a burger to nibble in the car, how will you serve it?"

At that point, you could hear a French fry drop. But the marketing people realized it wasn't their problem. It was now a question for the product development people.

The product development people were all long-distance runners who had overdosed on carbs and just didn't have the heart for this problem (so to speak). Many of these people had been fired from McDonald's for spearheading the low-fat burger, which lasted twelve days in central Indiana and is now on display at the Muncie Museum of History.

"Why don't we use two slices of tomato to wrap the sandwich in?" suggested one product development person.

"No," said Harvey, "tomato slices are wet and slippery. And messy. Not to mention seedy. That won't work."

Another suggested shoveling the whole thing into a bowl so it could be eaten like popcorn.

"No, no!" said Harvey. "Let's wrap the whole mess in lettuce."

"Oh, YUCK!" said the senior VP. "No one will eat that. We'd be better off putting the whole thing in the blender and making a shake out of it."

The veeps all looked at one another. Could that work? Had anyone ever tried it?

Harvey convinced the veeps to go with the lettuce. Then the research people got involved. They proved that if you eat a hamburger with pickles, onion, lettuce, tomato, ketchup, mustard, and mayonnaise, but no bun, every day for a month, you will lose five pounds.

But what would you expect, when the whole thing ends up in your lap instead of your mouth?

Harvey suggested using bibb lettuce. Even the veeps didn't laugh.

You either, huh?

That's Debatable

I watched the first 2004 presidential debate and I was struck by how much work must have been involved to take all the fun and excitement out of the event. I assume it was a committee who did this. No one person could mess up something that important so perfectly.

The next day I read that there were thirty-two pages of rules that both Republican and Democratic party officials agreed to follow. When I saw the rules, I wondered why there wasn't a similar manual for couples, using the same guidelines: RULES OF DEBATE FOR MARRIED PEOPLE. Here are a few guidelines, right from the Presidential Debate Handbook:

No Risers or Platforms

My wife and I are about the same height, but in high heels she towers over me, giving her an unfair psychological advantage when we argue. No wonder I never win. I'd rather debate Mitch Daniels than Mary Ellen.

No Questions to Your Opponent Except Rhetorical Ones

Perfect. Hey, that's the way we argue already:
"Is that any way to make a bed?"
"Is that what you call a pot roast?"
"Where does all our money go?"
"You don't think you're playing golf today, do you?

No Props or Charts

I'm not sure I agree with this one. It's much more effective with Mary Ellen if I wave a few L.S. Ayres bills in front of her face while I complain that we're not keeping to the budget. On the other hand, if my wife ever finds those dry cleaning receipts for my Wrangler jeans, it will come back to haunt me.

An Objective Moderator

Of all my neighbors, I'd pick Norm. The other people in the 'hood seem to like my wife better than me, but Norm I think would be the fairest

and most nonpartisan. Norm likes to borrow my
snow blower.

Two Identical Dressing Rooms

My wife's bathroom has a full-length mirror, a
built-in hair dryer, a spa tub, a stall shower, and
a walk-in closet. Except for the toilets, our bath-
rooms have nothing in common.

Your Own Makeup Arrangements

My wife has a dozen lipsticks, four mascaras,
three eyebrow pencils, and moisturizers for every
season. I have one bottle of Just for Men. I can't
out-debate someone with that much firepower.

No Roaming the Stage

Let's say that Mary Ellen is in the upstairs master bathroom yelling at me for leaving the toilet
seat up and I'm downstairs yelling about how
she parked on my side of the garage. She would
not be allowed to wander downstairs, enter the
garage, and get in my personal space to argue.
However, I don't think a rule like this would
stop her. It certainly didn't stop Al Gore.

The Studio Audience May Not Applaud

How are you supposed to know how you're
doing in an argument if there aren't lots of people

reacting? That's why after twenty-five years of marriage I can't win a quarrel. No feedback. After the debate, Kerry and Bush probably both thought they won. They probably asked their wives. That has never worked for me.

The Debate Begins and Ends with a Handshake

Never in twenty-five years have my wife and I started a disagreement with a handshake. And we never ended with one. I think a good bear hug works best. Maybe I'm more politically insightful than most, but I was dead-on when I predicted there would be very little hugging between Bush and Kerry after their final debate.

Backing the Space Program

CNN reported that the European Space Agency was looking for seven hundred women who would be willing to spend the next three months on their backs. That was their exact words, so please don't write me any nasty notes. My first thought (okay, not my first thought) was that the European Space Agency is in no position to put women in that position.

If you look at the people who have been sent into space, you don't see a lot of native-born Italians or Greeks. The French have never sent anyone to the moon. Come to think of it, France has never even sent anyone to Iraq.

The purpose of all this, of course, is to do research on how well women adapt to space flight, during which they are flat on their backs, staring up into...uh...space.

The agency had some stringent pre-qualifications. First, the women had to be self-starters. I'm no rocket scientist, but if you're looking for women who want to do nothing for three months but lounge around in bed, you're not going to get a lot of highly motivated people.

According to the CNN report, the women have to remain horizontal and are not allowed to tilt their head except to eat or watch a new episode of *Survivor*.

Bathing has to be done while reclining, which, in case the agency is not thinking that far ahead, is going to be murder on the sheets. I'm sure someone has already thought of this.

In the job description, women were informed that they would experience weightlessness periodically throughout the three-month period. This piqued the interest of several hundred French models who aspire to that sensation daily. The agency recruiters also favored the models because they had runway experience.

Eating during this entire period will be restricted to only those foods you can get into the side of your mouth without dribbling onto the expensive titanium ceiling tiles.

Family visitation is limited to weekends. All guests must maintain a vertical position, say the rules. HMMM ... there was a sign just like that in the elevator of my dorm at George Washington University in 1967.

As I finish this column, I see that some preliminary results are already in, but I don't think it's the kind of data the ESA was hoping for:

- 600 out of 700 women have already reported that the ceiling of the space agency needs painting.

- 650 women want to go back to either their husband, their boyfriend, or their Atkins diet.

- 100 women want to know if there is any permanent work in this field and if there is a pension.

- And 75 women had a grievance about their benefit package, claiming they should get sick pay if they wake up in the morning too ill to stay in bed.

A sour note: One woman signed up for the study to get over a bad divorce and now claims she got a rotten bed during the experiment. She is now suing both her ex-husband and the agency for lack of support.

Missing Miss America

Yes, there she goes, Miss America. The ABC network has dumped the show. Ratings dwindled and the bookmakers in England found fewer and fewer people willing to bet one hundred pounds on who would win Miss Congeniality. Brits will usually bet on anything. This was a very bad sign.

I know TV. I know what makes a rotten show. I've done so many of them. The pageant producers should have taken a look at the highly rated TV shows, analyzed what made them successful, and stolen their ideas. It's embarrassing I have to tell them this.

Who Wants to be a Millionaire?

Take a lesson from this popular quiz program. Instead of inane questions to the Miss America contestants, like, "What is the best way to establish world peace?" or, "If you were on a desert island, what one book would you bring along?" how about a few tricky multiple choicers, like:

> *In the expression "It takes two to tango,"*
> *what does the word tango refer to?*
> 1. A fruit
> 2. A yoga position
> 3. A party game
> 4. A dance

This would build suspense when Miss North Dakota decides to use her lifeline and ask the audience. She'll have to take into account that not one person in the crowd made the grueling trip from Bismarck—and that most of the people are pulling for the babe from Florida.

Survivor

The *Survivor* people got it right. Human qualities like greed, jealousy, spite, and hatred are paraded in front of the camera. That stuff sells. The Miss America pageant has just as much greed, jealousy, and hatred, but it's all behind the scenes. How stupid is that? Let's see how Miss Idaho stuck potatoes in her bra to look bigger. Or how Miss New York paid Miss New Jersey's brother to eliminate Miss New Hampshire.

The Mole

They could learn from this popular drama. You must have some mystery to capture people's attention. Include one cross-dresser as a Miss America contestant. But which one? People all over the country would be saying, "Yes, they are all lovely, but one of them is really Mister America." People may guess it's Miss Connecticut—no doubt thrown off by the faint remains of a mustache.

American Idol

Does it take a nuclear physicist to figure out that people really don't care who wins? They just want to insult the losers. That was Bert Parks's problem. If only Bert had asked "Are those your legs or are you standing behind a piano?" Just one remark like that and Bert would still have his job (if he weren't dead) and Miss America would be killing *The Bachelorette* in the ratings.

The Apprentice

The problem with the contest was that once the forty-nine losers were purged, it was back to being dental hygienists and manicurists and social workers. BOR-rrring. If Donald Trump were the host, he could say "You're fired," and offer all the losers a job dealing blackjack in French Lick. Why am I not getting paid for these ideas?

Desperate Housewives

Why is this show a hit? The title. The title! If it were *The Teri Hatcher Show* or *Life on Wisteria Lane*, you'd all be watching Animal Planet. It doesn't take five men in suits from Madison Avenue to tell you that when you change the name of the hamburger plate to chopped steak, you attract a bigger audience. Let's change *Miss America* to *Desperate Beauty Queens*. Watch the ratings soar.

I hope that *Miss America* finds a home on one of the cable networks. It's the kind of wholesome, tasteful, family-oriented viewing I enjoy. I just hope it's not up against *Fear Factor*.

McDriver

Have you read about this guy who wants to visit every McDonald's restaurant in America—all thirteen thousand of them—before he dies? This strikes me as a good idea because I wouldn't want to be inhaling a large order of fries when his family drags out the body.

He thinks he can do this in about two years, assuming he gets his food quickly and moves on to each next golden arch. This calculation requires that he avoid ordering from his car. Signs like: PARKING FOR DRIVE-THROUGH CUSTOMERS ONLY are a good indication of why. Special orders are also out of the question. McDonald's, I've heard, is considering offering free movie tickets for people who want a Quarter Pounder with no pickles, just so the wait doesn't seem so long.

Recently, I wrote a column about another guy who

has eaten two Big Macs every day for twenty years. This has put him in the *Guinness Book of World Records*, right next to a genius who ate an entire Schwinn bike. The *Guinness* people like to group things that are similar. I think you get the picture. By the way, the guy who ate the bike took twenty years to complete his feat also, savoring every piece of rubber tire over two decades. "Do you want spokes with that?"

There must be something about McDonald's that brings out all the glory seekers. Where are all the Burger King, KFC, and Taco Bell record-holders? I'd hate to think their accomplishments are going unnoticed. Some fast food junkies underestimate their abilities. What a waste of talent.

But back to our McDonald's friend. According to a report on National Public Radio, this character also holds another distinction. In one twenty-four-hour period, he ate in thirteen different McDonald's, a record that was just begging to be broken. To do this amazing feat in one day, he had to drive almost ten square blocks. This likens our hero to Lewis and Clark, except those guys probably ate better.

I admire people who have a goal in life. I mean here's a guy who probably just tired of performing the same routine surgical procedure every day and decided to devote his life to a real quest—something he could tell his grandkids about.

And there's still more to the story. He wants to

write a book about his experiences. He believes that sitting in McDonald's gives him a unique insight into American culture. I look forward to a time in my life when I can devote my leisure hours to the pursuit of some higher intellectual goal. A research project like this will distinguish me from other retirees who simply squander their time traveling in Europe, working with disadvantaged kids, volunteering in local hospitals, or raising money for United Way. And I'd like to get in *Guinness*, also. For example, I'd like to:

1. Go back and read all the *Nickel Traders* I've missed over the past twenty years.

2. At 5 A.M., knock on the front door of everyone who has a "welcome" mat and see if they really mean it.

3. In one summer, eat an elephant ear at every state fair. Wait, that's only fifty ears. Okay, every county fair, too.

4. Drive cross-country and have my oil changed at every ten-minute oil place. Then write an article for *Consumer Reports* on how I got hoodwinked into three thousand new air filters and six hundred wiper blades.

5. Go to every chiropractor in America and see if just one will say, "I've looked at the X-rays and I don't think there's anything wrong with your back."

6. Visit every White Castle in America. Order one burger. Then snap a photo of the guy's expression at the counter.

7. Test drive a new car. Drive the car due west and at the next dealership, leave the "borrowed" car while you drive one of their new vehicles. Work your way westward with this technique. By the time you reach L.A., you will have stolen about two thousand cars. If that doesn't get you in *Guinness* (and jail), nothing will.

That's enough for one retirement. I need to find a few moments just for myself.

Sick Humor

I don't think there's any question that laughter is God's special gift to humans. Other animals make tools, communicate, experience jealousy, and live in social groups. But only humans can laugh. That ability (plus mowing the lawn once a week) is what separates us from the hairy beast. Although in my neighborhood, you do see many hairy beasts mowing the lawn.

So you can imagine how thrilled I was to accept an invitation to speak to The Laughter Club, a monthly get-together at St. Vincent Hospital of staff and patients to experience the joys and therapeutic effects of laughing. What could possibly be better than a club where the purpose is to stand around giggling, guffawing, and chuckling? I'm a big fan of snickering also, but I sense this might be a bit mean-spirited for this group.

I work very hard during my speeches to get people to laugh. Here is a group of people predisposed to laugh, eager to laugh. Laughter is their mission. This was too good to be true. In fact, it wasn't true. Not any longer. The laughter is over.

I received a call from St. Vincent Hospital informing me that the Laughter Club had been cut, axed, eliminated, pink-slipped. Why?

"Budget cuts, Dick. It's a fact of life. Budget cuts."

BUDGET CUTS? How expensive could a Laughter Club be? Once a month, fifteen people get together for lunch and chuckle their way through their tuna on whole wheat. You gotta wonder how much money is being saved by axing this monthly activity. There's no labor, no capital investment. ZERO. Let's face it: If fifteen people yukking it up once a month in an empty room is putting you over budget, you need some ENRON people in there to tickle the accountants.

Don't hospital people know how to cut a budget? EKGs, EEGs, MRIs. There's got to be some fat in those budgets. Why are they taking this out on people who just want to laugh? There is something un-American about this. I'm sorry, you can't celebrate Bob Hope's one hundredth birthday and cut the Laughter Club in the same year. You can't give Jerry Seinfeld a Lifetime Achievement Award in comedy and cut the legs out from under the Laughter Club. (You *could* cut their neckties in half. Now that would be funny!)

I think I am going to start my own laughter club. And just to prove how inexpensively it can be done, I'm going to show you my budget. After some consultation with Clare, my accountant, we have put together this comprehensive estimate of expenditures based on twenty people in the club, one hour per meeting, once a month, for ten years, with continuous laughter.

NEW LAUGHTER CLUB BUDGET

Room Rental: FREE (my house)
Refreshments: Bring your own
Jokes: Bring someone else's

TOTAL COST: NOTHING

I know this is brilliant and I guess I can't expect people in modern medicine who are dealing with two-million-dollar CAT scanners to be as financially savvy as me, but I do hope they will consider this and reinstate the Laughter Club.

When St. Vincent heard I was writing an article about this, they weren't happy....

"Dick, you shouldn't be making fun of financial cuts. Fiscal problems are not a laughing matter."

"They better not be. Apparently, that could get expensive."

Mega-Bites

I went into a local gas station the other day where I always get my breakfast bagel and morning coffee. Because I can't taste the difference between their Colombian, Hazelnut, and French Roast, it's the easiest decision I make all day. Of course, at 5:00 A.M., I can't tell the difference between Larry, Moe, and Curly.

I ordered my traditional bagel with cream cheese.

I got the bagel and I got the cream cheese, but they took most of the tradition out of it.

Normally, I banter back and forth with the woman behind the counter. She tells me what's wrong with my TV segment and then I get into a lather by telling her how much better bagels were when I was growing up in New York. We keep the conversation very cordial, because there are usually four police officers sitting within earshot. I don't want my passion to be misunderstood as hostility. That would never have happened to me in New York.

That morning, as I considered trying the low-carb, cardboard-flavored bagel, I was told by a young man behind the counter that all orders must now be punched into a computer. By the customer!

"But I'm the only one in the store," I said to the clerk. "The police aren't even here yet."

"Sorry, sir, but that's how we operate now. Please place your order on the screen. It's really very simple."

"Yeah, sure. That's what they said about Turbo Tax. Look, all I want is a bagel and a cup of coffee. I don't need a reminder at five in the morning that I am computer illiterate."

Then I looked at the screen:

WHAT KIND OF BAGEL DO YOU WANT?

    ◯   **DO YOU WANT IT SLICED?**

    ◯   **DO YOU WANT IT TOASTED?**

WHAT WOULD YOU LIKE ON THE BAGEL?

PLEASE TOUCH SCREEN NOW TO MAKE YOUR SELECTION

Oh, dear. I only like the cream cheese spread on the bottom half of the bagel. I looked everywhere. There was no place to register that preference. At home, whenever I am unsure where to press something on my computer, my friend Ben happily comes over for sixty dollars an hour to explain it to me.

Then I had to choose a coffee. One of them was Sultry Sumatra, which was described on the computer screen as "voluptuously round." My friend downloaded something like this on a computer at the public library and they took away his card.

There is something very wrong with this new concept. I come from New York, where if you buy a bagel from someone, you have established a special relationship with that person. I think this started in the Old Testament and goes back to 1000 B.C.C.E. (Before Cream Cheese, Even).

"Why can't I order directly from you?" I asked the clerk.

"It prevents any mistakes, sir. This way you won't walk away with onion when you wanted asiago."

"But what if I punch the wrong screen name by mistake?"

"Then we would have proof that it was your fault."

I don't know about you, but I seldom say pumpernickel when I mean to say jalapeno. It's not the kind of slip you make, no matter how careless you are with your speech.

I didn't buy a bagel and coffee that day, and I'd suggest that you also protest by never ordering your breakfast on a computer. Getting a bagel should be a personal experience, not a high-tech one. Look, I don't want to shmear that place's reputation, but any way you slice it, they are spreading the wrong message.

Heard of Cows

Just when you thought that technology had reached its zenith, just when you thought the scientific world couldn't come up with anything new, just when you thought that anything worth inventing had been invented—just when you thought all this, someone invented a machine that can tell you what cows are thinking.

Who knew a moo could ring true? Not many do. Did you?

Dr. Seuss, eat your heart out.

By the way, this device (it's actually a collar with a tiny video read-out) will also tell you what dogs are thinking. But what a waste of money. Dogs want to eat or go for a walk.

So if I were you, I'd save the cash and whenever your dog barks, toss him a hunk of sirloin. Even if you guessed wrong, you'll have a happy dog. (But maybe a wet carpet.)

This cow thing has got me intrigued. I'm no different from you. We have all wondered what a cow could be thinking. Goats? Chickens? Sheep? Who cares? But cows? That's news we can use. Moos we can use? Whatever.

Let's not ever forget the tremendous influence that cows have on us. Every day we all feel the full force of the bovine linguistic paradigm in our lives. Even those who eschew meat can't resist its power. Not to mention those who chew it.

Consider:

- Being put out to pasture
- Having a cow
- Milking something for all it's worth
- Beefing up
- Cow-towing
- A bunch of bull
- Cowlick
- Cowering
- Power steering
- Udderly ridiculous

And we would be remiss if we did not mention the common malady suffered by all who drive their cars past a meadow: bovilexia, which is the urge to open the window and yell MOO!

But back to what cows are thinking.

When I drive by a field and see cows just standing around mooing, I wonder what a moo can mean. Cows have a lot of time to think—more so than dogs, who occasionally have family obligations. But cows, even when being milked, are pretty much free to think about all manner of things. What do cows think about? I'd give a Big Mac to know.

Look what happens to most of us when we just have hours to drift off in our own little worlds. You know how dangerous that can get. You can get yourself in serious trouble when you have too much time to think. Pablo Picasso was happy as a clam painting fruit in a bowl twenty-four hours a day. Then he got ahead of schedule and had some extra time to just think. I think you get my point.

Well, if humans can get themselves in a pickle by just pondering, imagine what a cow can come up with to think about twenty hours a day. Here are a few things they found that cows say and what they mean:

• MOOOOOOO: I hate that "Got Milk" commercial. Let's clear this up right now. I got the milk. But you've been stealing the milk.

• MOOO MOOO: What's this about cow tipping? Twenty years serving milk, and I've never seen a penny.

• MMMMOOOOO: Take us off the Gateway Computer boxes or talk to our attorneys.

• MMMOO: You think it's easy being a cow? You try chewing the same thing for twenty years.

• MOOOOOOOOOOOOOOOOOOOOOOOO OOOOOOOOOOOOOOOOOOOOOOOO: I'm in heat, but this doesn't last very long, so hurry up. Too late. Sorry.

That's pretty much it. I could go on, but my dog just told me that it's getting late and he wants to take a walk now so he can get home in time for Animal Planet and then take a nap in front of the fire before he goes upstairs to bed.

I think that's what he said. Either that, or he's hungry.

How to Read a Redhead

This is one of those "I swear I'm not making this up" beginnings, but here it is: The newspaper reported last week that according to a researcher at the University of Louisville, it takes 20 percent more anesthesia to knock out a redhead.

I mean, why don't they just write my entire humor essay for me? This is too easy. I'm embarrassed to accept money for turning this one in.

According to the article, this little piece of research was very expensive because it is very difficult to tell when a person is really anesthetized. The only thing that researchers found more difficult was determining in Kentucky who is really a redhead. (I wanted to get the Kentucky joke out of my system early so I can go on to better stuff.)

By the way, my wife is a redhead, but she's already a

knockout. (I also wanted to get that in because her birthday is around the corner and this was good chance to score some points.)

Why would someone study something like this? Where would someone get the idea that hair color has anything to do with what's inside a human being? Gee, the next thing you know, some jerk will start telling jokes about blondes. I know it's crazy, but you never know.

But let's get back to this redhead thing again. Researchers asked brunettes and redheads to voluntarily allow themselves to be hooked up to some electrodes so scientists could shock them with a gradually increasing intensity while at the same time upping the amount of anesthesia. The idea was to see who would complain about the pain first, the brunette or the redhead. In other words, who needed more anesthesia.

This same experiment, which I thought had been outlawed by some international treaty after WWII, apparently proved that redheads are either total wimps or are smart enough to quickly say, "Hey, knock it off you big PhD hillbilly, or I'll take off these wires and wrap them around your neck." The scientists did not report this, of course, because I guess they didn't want to give electrical shock experimentation a bad name.

By the way, both groups of women voluntarily agreed to this experiment for a small stipend, which does suggest that women with any color hair from Louisville are willing to do anything for a buck. In Kentucky, that kind of publicity is great for tourism.

I didn't show my wife the article because I wanted to do a little independent study myself. My friend's wife is a brunette, so he and I came up with some test situations. I hate to admit this but based on an entire weekend of exhaustive research, I discovered there really are some differences between redheads and brunettes. At least from the husband's standpoint.

According to my research, a man with a redheaded wife:

1. Requires a 20 percent more expensive restaurant to get out of the doghouse.
2. Needs 15 percent more pleading to play golf on a Sunday morning.
3. Will be 12 percent later for the symphony.
4. Is 14 percent more likely to say the wrong thing at a party.
5. Will tell 80 percent fewer jokes about people with freckles.
6. Will spend 35 percent more time saying to clerks at Christmastime, "My wife can't wear that color."
7. If he's smart, is 100 percent less likely to use the word "fiery" in front of her when she gets angry.

Before you jump to any conclusions, please remember that these findings are based only on two women in Indianapolis. Your results may vary.

Cookie Monsters

Did you hear about this? Some nut was trying to sue Kraft, the company that makes Oreo cookies. He said that Oreos were slowly killing him. So what's the problem? Quite frankly, this is how I've always wanted to die.

I'd like to say that I knew this lawsuit was coming, but I had no clue. Fig Newtons, yes. A tooth could get caught in one. A Fig Newton is a lawsuit waiting to happen. Ginger snaps: very dangerous, mostly from the whiplash. But Oreo cookies? Never. You sue the Oreo cookie people and the next thing you know the Reese's Peanut Butter Cup people will be in the slammer. This is a very slippery slope. Even for peanut butter.

This guy was upset because an Oreo contains hydrogenated oils known as trans fats, which shocked me. I thought Trans Fats was an airline for overweight people.

Apparently these trans fats can kill you, although the

Kraft company claims that 450 billion Oreos have been eaten in the last one hundred years and no autopsy has ever listed the cause of death as Oreo cookies. Now, that's a record Kraft can be proud of. I'm not sure even the Reese's people can make that statement.

I've been eating Oreo cookies for fifty years. I think we all know the ritual. You get a huge glass of cold milk, and twenty or thirty Oreos, and then you start twisting them apart. Some people eat the side with cream frosting first, some just eat the frosting, and others start with the all-chocolate wafer. Some dip the cookie in milk; some guzzle the milk after the cookie.

How can you sue a company that has given you so many wonderful options in your life?

So, did this guy have a case? Unlike cigarettes, where a warning is clearly emblazoned on the package, there is no cookie admonition anywhere on the package or on the cookie.

Considering how people eat Oreos, I would suggest that inside the cookie, right in the vanilla cream, the Kraft people print in eighteen-point type:

> **The Surgeon General** has determined that eating Oreo cookies over an entire lifetime can raise your triglycerides and affect the critical balance between your good and bad cholesterol.

I don't think the warning will deter anyone, but it will mean they will have to make the cookie bigger, which is something I have been advocating for a long time.

The Kraft people said they would vigorously fight the lawsuit. They admit their cookies have trans fats but they claim they are already testing alternatives. Alternatives is a code word for "a healthy but tasteless substitute."

When McDonald's said they were looking for an alternative to their fatty hamburger, they came up with a soy burger. Research showed that two out of three people who ate the burgers loved them. That was the problem. In six months only three people ate them. The rest is history.

Look, I'm all for nutritional food (actually, I'm not, but my wife thought I should say that), but I do think they should leave the Oreo cookie people alone. If this guy wants to sue someone, I'd suggest suing the company that makes Slim Jims. A Slim Jim is 98 percent fat, has no vitamins or minerals, and makes you want to drink a six-pack of beer. On second thought, let's cut them some slack, also.

How about those cauliflower and broccoli farmers who have been getting away with murder for years? Did you know that people are dipping that stuff in breading and deep frying it?

Those farmers better have some pretty good lawyers.

Milk Duds

There's a column in the local paper written by a wine expert. In this week's column, the headline is, "Who Says Deck Wines Have to be White?"

Well, you could have blown me over with a straw. I was thunderstruck, as Mark Twain used to say. Don't tell me after decades of red on the deck that the protocol has changed, that the rules have relaxed. Is there no shame?

By the way, what's a deck wine?

Wine people always claim that they're not snooty. Their proof here is that they will now allow us to guzzle Merlot instead of sipping Chablis AND, hold on to your corks, you can do it on your deck. I ask again, where is the shame? I also ask again, what's a deck wine?

I have never had any problems picking wine. I pick my favorite color (red), then my favorite vintage

(October), and then my favorite topper (twist off), and voilá: the perfect wine. Yes, wine selection is a breeze. But milk is another story altogether.

I see people making egregious milk errors all the time. They make no distinction between 1 percent, 2 percent, whole, and skim. I saw someone the other day sipping 1 percent out of a straw while eating a Little Debbie cake. Where was this guy raised? Probably not on a farm, where dairymen still rue the day that someone wanted to skim the cream off the top of their milk and sell it in a compromised state.

Many people nowadays pick one kind of milk and stick with it. They drink it with everything. I'm getting queasy just talking about it. I call it the homogenization of America. And it's just the beginning of a slippery slope. Continue this and someday we'll all be put out to Pasteur.

In my house, we keep all four types of milk in the fridge and I have established some very strict rules about what goes with what. I would no more let my son drink 1 percent with a Fig Newton than I would drink a Miller Lite with a Twinkie or a Budweiser with a spinach soufflé.

Since no one else has stepped forward, allow me to be your milk maven, providing a blueprint for your future selection of milk. If you have gone through life thinking that one milk fits all, I am going to change all that. You're going to owe me big time. I have no patience for people who don't understand this. I am lactose intolerant.

- **Whole:** Recommended for newborn babies who need a high fat content. And adults with a full bag of Oreo cookies or a plate of brownies.

- **2 percent:** For Rice Krispies, Shredded Wheat, Corn Flakes, and Total. With Pop-Tarts, peanut butter sandwiches, Fig Newtons, ginger snaps, oatmeal cookies, and Little Debbie any-thing. Also to lighten coffee.

- **1 percent:** On sugar pops, sugar smacks, Froot Loops, Cocoa Puffs, Frosted Flakes or to guzzle right from the bottle.

- **Skim:** As a shampoo and to get out wine and blood stains. Not recommended for human con-sumption.

Well, that's it for this week. You might have thought this column was stupid, but I know you're going to tape it to your fridge door.

Take This Job and Love It

How can you train for a long life? According to a recent survey, the city you live in makes a big difference.

The annual list of best cities to live in was recently published and the number one pick was Pittsburgh, which was kind of a strange choice because four groups of people disagreed with this poll:

1. The people who had never been to Pittsburgh
2. The people who had been to Pittsburgh
3. The people who lived in Pittsburgh
4. The people who used to live in Pittsburgh

But the newest list I've seen published takes the cake (cake, by the way, is the second-most requested dessert). This list ranks the best jobs in America. If you love your job, they say, you will live longer. In order to make this assessment, the authors took into account job satisfaction, money, stress, room for advancement, benefits, and whether there was casual Friday.

The number-one job in America is biologist. I think the results you get on a survey like this depend on who picks up the phone. The biologist at Edy's ice cream would probably have a different take on her job than the biologist at the CIA who juggles vials of smallpox. Hey, I'm no expert on data collection, but I think I have a point.

One of the criteria was job stress. The top five jobs with the least stress included financial advisor and forklift operator. I wouldn't lie about this. (The two top things lied about are sex and money.)

Whoever did this research has apparently not talked to a financial advisor in the last twelve financial quarters. Some advisors are so stressed that they are now standing in front of forklift operators hoping to be put out of their misery.

The highest stress job was president of the United States. Why? There is no job security and it pays about 90 percent less than a pro basketball player. This is why only about six people vie for this job every four years. Maybe if we increased the pay and threw in a few extra health benefits and a free agent clause, we'd get more interest in the job.

Corporate executive was ranked as having very high

stress. This comes from the tremendous responsibilities you have to shoulder coupled with the anxiety of not knowing how the parole board will rule.

Two other high-stress jobs were taxi driver and racecar driver. This is understandable. Travelling at high speeds, making hairpin turns, putting your life at risk, and the possibility of killing others is very stressful. Racecar drivers also have a risky job.

The worst-rated job was lumberjack. Lumberjack? I've never met an unhappy lumberjack. What's not to be happy about? You're outdoors, you're exercising, there are no meetings. You can wear the same shirt every day. Maybe if they threw in formal Friday, it would help things. And there's no stress. Oh, occasionally there's an environmentalist in a tree you're chopping down, but I don't think that would faze most lumberjacks.

Anyway, lists like these are on my list of things that annoy me. Reading them stresses me out. I just feel better when I'm listless.

Pumped Up

You must be kind of bummed out because of the high gas prices. The good news is that if you work for a company that pays you 37.5 cents a mile to operate your own car, you could drive sixty miles per hour for twenty-four hours and make almost five hundred dollars a day.

Of course, that would require several visits to a gas station every day. It's funny, but oil companies don't like the term "gas station." They used to prefer service station, but they don't have any service anymore and there's a limit even to what the oil companies can say with a straight face. Service stations do have bread, milk, peach iced tea, pizza, lottery tickets, butane tanks, cheerleader calendars, and kindling wood.

Excellent service, including someone to pump your gas, is only a distant memory for baby boomers like me. When I was young and virile and could pump my own gas, they did it for me. Since 1997, I have had two bad knees, a bad elbow, and I've become lazy. Now I'm supposed to pump my own. This was very poor planning on everyone's part.

I have other complaints. No matter how many years I drive the same car, I still don't have a clue what side my gas tank is on. I drive into the station and try to look in my side-view mirror, but I can't see the gas cap. So I take a chance and pull up to the pump. WRONG SIDE. Then I get back in the car and drive completely around the pump to the other side. WRONG SIDE AGAIN. I look around. If this were an IQ test, my application to Mensa would be under some serious scrutiny. I don't remember this happening thirty years ago.

And the gas pump is always asking me questions requiring a response.

Do you want to pay inside?

Do you want a car wash?

Do you want a receipt?

Do you want a Krispy Kreme doughnut?

But I can never find the right button. Is it just me?

Milk, by the way, is $2.39 a gallon. This really has nothing to do with service stations, but I'm trying to get my mind off the high gas prices.

Milk prices are also very erratic, which is perplexing because cows are not nearly as involved in geopolitical events as the Arab oil nations. I'm not sure what factors are driving the price increase. What would happen if companies had to drill for milk?

First of all, it would be tough on the employees of all the Village Pantries and 7-Elevens who would have to get up on a ladder every morning and change the milk prices.

WHOLE MILK: $2.39 and $\frac{9}{10}$ cents per gallon

2 PERCENT MILK: $2.41 and $\frac{9}{10}$ cents per gallon

CHOCOLATE MILK: $2.45 and $\frac{9}{10}$ cents per gallon

The result, of course, would be milk wars in America. Sounds pretty serious compared to milk fights, and although they don't have the same sense of gravity, it does bring back memories of life in the high school cafeteria.

High milk prices could have a serious effect on the birth rate. Babies are fun, but they are milk guzzlers. To have more than one or two would be unpatriotic.

By the way, I figured out last night that the coffee I get with my gas every morning would be about fourteen dollars a gallon (and the gas is not too far behind!).

I hope that makes you feel better.

My First McStep

I read the other day that McDonald's had come up with a concept that is going to revolutionize the fast food business. I tried to imagine what kind of improvements could possibly improve on something that is already perfect. Okay, there are a few things I'd like to see fixed. What if they:

1. Took the word "fast" seriously?
2. Put the right order in the right bag?
3. Improved the acoustics over the intercom so that "Do you want fries with that?" is not "dwanzfrifhfhffiresiddat?"

Sorry, those improvements are still in the future. Apparently, there was a greater consumer demand for something else. Now, when you buy a Big Mac, double order of fries, and a shake, you get a free stepometer. When I heard about this I was just so excited that I ran out and got a dictionary so I could see what a stepometer was.

Brace yourself: A stepometer counts the number of steps you take when you walk. The idea here is that if you know how many steps you take each day, it will help you lose weight. We'll take a short McBreak now while we all go "HUH?"

I did some research and there are only two recorded cases of someone actually taking a walk after eating fast food. One was Bernie Featherston of Atlanta who walked from McDonald's over to Arby's because he likes horseradish sauce on his fries. And there's Beth Cutler of Peoria, who bought the new M&M Blizzard at Dairy Queen, then walked over to Weight Watchers so she could drink it in front of the window right before she turned in her resignation.

In the old days, fast food establishments included toys with your order to appeal to the kids. But the new marketing approach is to give some incentive to adults as well. Apparently, McDonald's commissioned a five-million-dollar study and it was determined that a lot of those kids who eat at McDonald's grow up to be adults. That seemed to surprise the McDonald's executives. Sure, fast food is bad for you, but not that bad.

Bob Greene, Oprah's personal trainer, has been promoting this stepometer. He claims that the average person takes only 2,500 steps a day. (This number would be much higher if half the people in America weren't in bed watching *Oprah* in the middle of the day or reading one of the books she is hawking.)

I think this is just the beginning. Here are a couple of concepts that might also appeal to the masses:

How about a biteometer? This would tell a person how many bites he has taken while eating at McDonald's. That's the kind of immediate feedback that can help someone decide on subsequent trips if he has enough time for a Big Mac or has to settle for a double cheeseburger.

Or a tape measure with every meal at Taco Bell? Eat a burrito and an enchilada. Then wrap that baby around you and see if you have room for the Gordita Supreme. That's the kind of data you can really use.

Now that I am getting closer to my senior years, I'd like a little portable hypertension kit with my lunch. Then, when I get back to my house with a filet of fish sandwich instead of the chicken club I ordered, I can test my blood pressure to see just how ticked off I am.

Judging Poetry

Judge J. Michael Eakin of Pennsylvania was in the news this week. Apparently, the judge likes to dispense justice with a flair. Instead of the normal ruling from the bench, Judge Eakin hands down decisions that rhyme. Here's an example, based on a young woman suing a man for giving her a fake diamond engagement ring:

> *A groom must respect*
> *Matrimonial pandemonium*
> *When his spouse finds he's given her*
> *A cubic zirconium.*
> *Given their history and Pygmalion relation*
> *I find her reliance was with justification.*

Ya just gotta love this guy. Talk about poetic justice.

Wouldn't we all live in a better, more peaceful world if all our exchanges were in rhyme?

Like when a cop stops you for speeding:

> *Sorry, Officer James O'Grady*
> *For clocking me at more than eighty.*
> *There's one thing I need to mention:*
> *My cell phone caused my inattention.*
> *That and coffee and a VCR*
> *I forgot that I was in a car.*

Great, huh? What police officer wouldn't just send you on your way?

How about if caught shoplifting? If only Winona had the poetic muse:

> *I know it looks kinda shifty*
> *But I see it as wisely thrifty.*
> *Why pay for stuff that I'll take back?*
> *The fur coat's white, I needed black.*
> *And so I make this last appeal*
> *Please shop here, the stuff's a steal.*

How about if the IRS calls you in and questions one of your deductions? These guys just love a good poem.

My name is Bunny, exotic dancer,
Looking for a cash enhancer.
As you can see from my lovely form
My deductions are not the norm.
May I deduct my thong bikini?
You're so cute, don't be a meanie.
My clothes are sexy and oh so soft
And on my taxes, I'll take them off.

You have just hit a guy in the parking lot with your car. If ever you needed a rhyme...

I may be wrong, don't be offended
Was that your Lexus I just rear-ended?
At ninety grand, I'm sure your lender
Would love to see your crumpled fender.
Now here's a time of great decision
Who will attend to this collision?
Some will think it's just a stunt
The way your back seat's in the front.

He'll be laughing, so he'll settle out of court. But what if your wife finds lipstick on your collar? Not her lipstick, either.

I know you think that I'm pathetic
'Cause you found that strange cosmetic.
So, I think I'll be confessing

Not to cheating, but cross-dressing.
Late at night, I'm with no girly
After ten they call me Shirley.

And a final word to my readers:

This week's method that I chose
Was to avoid the boring prose.
Instead I treated you to rhyme
But thank the Lord, it's the last time.

Needs Improvement

I was at my storage unit the other day, rearranging my stuff. This is pretty much the same stuff that George Carlin talked about forty years ago in a famous comedy routine. In fact, it's the same stuff I was moving around when I first listened to that routine.

I shoved my eight-track deck under the Beta VCR and piled my old *Life* magazines alongside my Ford Pinto bumper, which was lodged against my stereo turntable, which was scraping against my Victrola, which may be an item you are not familiar with, but if you are, you now you know how old I am.

This kind of organizing requires a deft touch. You must be able to add items to the storage bin and then accept the fact that this will be the last time you will ever see any of this stuff.

Of course, you could throw stuff out, but then

you'd find out your old Monopoly game would have sold on eBay for five hundred dollars. Even more, if you weren't missing the "Get out of Jail Free" cards.

While rummaging through years of saved junk, I found an old report card dated 1957 from Roosevelt Elementary School. That was the year I spent sparring with Mrs. O'Connell, my fourth-grade teacher. I think she had a crush on my dad, because she sent a letter home to him every night. My father would then pretend it was about my behavior in class. But when he read the note I could see his face get all red, so I'm sure something was going on between them. My mother and father must have had a very open relationship because he would actually show the note to my mother.

In those days, kids were given either an N (needs improvement), an S (satisfactory), or an E (excellent). I tried to convince my parents that N meant nine out of ten. They didn't buy it.

This system made things simple for the teacher, yet I also rated editorial comments, because Mrs. O'Connell would scribble little notes in the margin, which seemed a bit over the top to me.

I would now, fifty years later, respond to each of those comments.

Dickie needs to exercise more self-control. He seems to think that being silly is a way to gain attention.

Dear Mrs. O'Connell,

I would like you to know that I have spent my adult life making people laugh. And I want to thank you because when I first discovered that this ticked you off, I knew I was on to something really cool.

Dickie has the messiest desk in the whole class. That must change.

Dear Mrs. O'Connell,

Thanks to you, I now have the neatest desk in the world. All my manila folders have typed labels and are in alphabetical order. Every pencil is sharpened and they all face in the same direction. You made me so compulsive about neatness and cleanliness, I didn't kiss a girl until I was twenty-four. Which reminds me—what was going on between you and my father?

Dickie's spelling is just atrocious. I keep telling him how important spelling will be when he grows up.

Deer Mrs. O'Connell,

You mite be surprised to here this, but no won nose I'm knot a grate speller because of Spell Check.

Well, I'm glad I got that off my chest. I'm going to mail my letter back to my old school, but I don't think Mrs. O'Connell will get it. She'd be about 110 years old and Roosevelt Elementary is now a high-rise condominium.

Ants in
the Pants

Big news in the world of medicine. It turns out that people who are couch potatoes spend more time on the couch than other people.

WOW! I always kind of suspected that, but no one wanted to pay me the big bucks for that information so I kept it to myself.

The researchers recruited ten mildly obese and ten lean people to wear special underwear that used technology developed for fighter jet control panels. Sensors were embedded in the subjects' undergarments, which then recorded their postures and movements every half-second, twenty-four hours a day, for ten days. Apparently it wasn't hard to get people to volunteer for this. I think the idea of having jet controls in your underwear was one of the attractions.

They called this apparatus a "movement monitor,"

which intrigued members of AARP until they found out what it was really measuring. Maybe there will be another study for the kind of information they are looking for.

The study found that people who are thin spend a lot of time in their lives just puttering around, not necessarily doing anything constructive, but just puttering around.

I am a putterer, myself. Not a putter—a putterer. Just like someone who stutters is a stutterer, I am a putterer.

Now I find out that my puttering is the explanation for why a person like me, who can eat an entire pepperoni and sausage pizza but who exercises very little, remains thin. Who knew?

According to the study, these movement monitors revealed that people can be divided into two groups: those who love to sit and those who are constantly moving.

My life has always been a moving experience. I seldom just sit. I eat standing up; I am on an exercise bike right now as I write this column; I read while walking up the stairs; I shake my leg up and down while at the dinner table or having a conversation with my wife. I check my e-mail forty times a day, which involves going up and down the basement steps each time.

Of course, I do like to watch TV, but I never lounge

on the couch. I'm either standing up in front of the TV ready to change the channel or running around the house looking for the remote. Or I'm looking for my cell phone. Or my keys.

I am the picture of hyperactivity. In the summer, hummingbirds gather at the window for inspiration.

My entire life, my mother, my wife, and my doctor have told me that my behavior was very troubling, that my nervousness would have a negative effect on my whole system, that it meant a shorter and less healthful life. "Calm down, relax," they would tell me. "You'll live longer." I'm glad I didn't listen to them. I'd be four hundred pounds heavier by now.

Today I went outside and checked my mailbox several times to see if the mail had come. My neighbors think I am a bit strange, but they do not understand the aerobic benefit of this activity. I don't blame them for thinking it odd.

But what better way to spend a Sunday?

Part 3

Ewe and I

(Stories about My Flock)

Thought-Provoking

My wife was bragging about me the other day. Mary Ellen teaches a course on advertising at Butler University and apparently she told her class that her husband was a divergent thinker.

There was some polite applause at her solid choice for a mate and more than a few coeds expressed hope that they would be so lucky in their own love lives.

When I first heard about it, I was so overjoyed, so appreciative, that I took my wife out for an expensive dinner, bought a pricey bottle of wine, and romanced her like I had never romanced her before. But it didn't work. I still didn't have any idea what a divergent thinker was. I tried prying it out of her....

"Mary Ellen, could you just give me a hint?"

"Well, Dick. I could give you lots of hints, but it wouldn't mean anything. You still wouldn't understand.

That's what makes you a divergent thinker. Clues don't help you. Even with clues, you're clueless."

"Huh?"

"You are not capable of taking a series of ideas and coming to a conclusion. That is convergent thinking. You, on the other hand, are a divergent thinker. In strict psychological terms you find it difficult to extrapolate a series of seemingly unrelated data and construct a viable conclusion based on the information in your purview. You can't focus on one correct answer. You are weak in inductive and deductive reasoning, inquiry, and logic."

"Please, what does this mean in English?"

"Dizzy, Dick. You are dizzy."

I thought about all the times I've forgotten where I parked the car, the fact that I can't read a map, that I can't follow directions in a manual, that I am always losing my keys, that I sometimes forget why I went to the store, or who I'm calling on the phone.

Okay, fine. I admit all this, but where does she come off calling me dizzy?

"Look, Dick," she continued, "as much as I love you, I don't think we should go to the movies together anymore. You never understand any of the plots. You start asking me dumb questions two minutes after we sit down."

"Well, sometimes you don't know the answers, either."

"That's because we are watching the previews, Dick. Then the movie starts and you ask me whether we know the couple in front of us, whether I have butter on my popcorn, why popcorn is so expensive, where we are going for dinner, in what other movie have we seen that actor, if next time we can sit farther back. All this while I'm trying to do something else."

"What are you doing that is so important?"

"Watching the movie, Dick. I am watching the movie."

"I didn't know you were that focused. Isn't that bad for your blood pressure?"

"Look, Dick, there are some advantages to being a divergent thinker. You probably could think of fifteen different ways to use a shoetree other than putting it in a shoe. I am sure that if we were shipwrecked on a deserted island you could find a way to use my undergarments to catch fish."

"Wow, and I was just beginning to get down on myself. Thanks for the pep talk."

"Focus, Dick, focus. You'll be a better person."

The last few days I've tried not to be dizzy. I have tried to focus on the task at hand. I've concentrated on everything around me and I have avoided being distracted by extraneous events. Most of all, I have committed myself to staying interested in what I am doing so that

Have a Heart

I have never been a big fan of Valentine's Day. I always give my wife a gift on her birthday, on Mother's Day, and on Christmas. I also give her a present every time our new dog eats a pair of her high-heeled shoes. I brought home a trinket just last month after I accidentally used her cashmere scarf to check the oil dipstick in my car. Don't ever accuse me of not being thoughtful.

I think the above is an adequate expression of my affection without my having to get up, get dressed, start the car in the dead of winter, and slowly make my way through the ice and snow just to prove to her she is my Valentine. She is. Why can't she just take my word for it?

But I'm no wimp. I did go to Marsh at halftime during the Super Bowl for nachos.

Unfortunately, Mary Ellen loves Valentine's Day. She knows how I suffer finding just the right card (romantic, but not goopy; sexy, but not dirty; funny, but not stupid). Last year I didn't have the patience to look, so I waited at the gift store until someone walked in who seemed like the kind of guy who might marry a woman like Mary Ellen. I waited until he looked at a card and laughed out loud. Then I bought that card. Unless it was a real lecherous laugh. I stopped giving those cards to Mary Ellen in 1983.

I had just about given up on the perfect gift when I saw something in the newspaper that changed everything. Finally, a gift that any woman would cherish. Get ready. I'm not making this up: bullet-hole decals for your car.

Here's another example of where you just want to slap yourself upside the head for not thinking of it. All the time I have wasted over the past twenty-five years going to spas for massage gift certificates and Victoria's Secret for sexy lingerie, I could have saved myself the trouble and just bought a dozen bullet-hole decals. It kinda makes a dozen roses seem almost thoughtless.

It gets better. You can pick out the caliber bullet you want. Do you want it to look like you were the victim of a drive-by shooting or do you want to do the Bonnie and Clyde fantasy thing? Maybe you want to cruise through a bad neighborhood and look like you belong. This is a very versatile gift.

Not only that—but unlike flowers, bullet decals are a great conversation starter. If a woman tells her friends at lunch on February 16 that her hubby plopped six roses in a vase for V-Day, the conversation will quickly turn to whether there is too much mayonnaise in the chicken salad.

But would Mary Ellen like fake bullet holes? I've bought things on eBay before that just didn't seem to fire up the romance. When Jesse Ventura's old wrestling trunks with his autograph on the seat were a major gift dud, I began to question if I really knew my wife's tastes. Isn't it funny how you can share a bed with someone for twenty-five years and not have a clue what they're really all about?

I think I'll hold off on the bullet holes until next year. Mary Ellen has been going through a kind of passive stage in her life. The last fifty-two years she has hated guns, despised football, and refused to watch a violent movie. I think I'll go back to roses.

I may even remove the thorns.

Kernel of Truth

After twenty-five years of togetherness, my wife and I have some serious questions about whether our relationship can really continue any longer when we have such a fundamental disagreement about one aspect of our marital life: popcorn.

From the moment we get in the car to go to the movies there is a disharmony in what might otherwise be considered a perfect union.

"You're not going to get popcorn this time, are you, Mary Ellen? We're going out for a very expensive dinner right after the movie."

"I have to. It's been a movie tradition for me since high school."

"So was necking in the balcony, but we've cut that out almost completely."

Once we reach the theater, the tension rises.

"Dick, I'll find a seat. You wait in line for the popcorn."

"Why do I have to wait in line? I don't want popcorn. And when I come into the movie theater you'll forget to look around for me and I'll walk aimlessly up and down the aisles while people stare at me and assume I'm all alone and have no one to sit with."

Of course, I do wait in line. I buy the popcorn and a drink.

"Why did you get the extra large, Dick? You know we can't eat all that."

"Because the extra large is only fifty cents more than the small and you get five times more popcorn. I already feel like I'm getting ripped off and I don't want them to get away with it. Did you know that popcorn used to be a quarter?"

"Yes, and the people in the films are talking now."

Another issue is butter and salt. My wife is a bit of a health nut so she avoids butter and salt. But popcorn with no butter and salt? You have to be kidding. Why not just buy a cheap clock radio, tear up the Styrofoam around the unit into tiny pieces, and put them into a bag. Enjoy. It'll taste the same.

And then there's eating the popcorn. My wife takes one piece from the top of the box with two fingers, then places the popcorn in her mouth where she lets it melt on her tongue. Mary Ellen claims this gets her into a rhythm to enjoy the movie. I believe this technique is practiced by alien life forms or possibly by members of a satanic cult in Utah. In my peripheral vision, I can see my wife's arm move up and down about 1,100 times during the movie. I don't remember films I've seen because I've been hypnotized through them.

Here's the right way to eat popcorn: Dig way down into the container, which spews popcorn all over people on either side of you. Take an entire handful, shake the kernels up in your fist like a pair of dice and throw several into your mouth at one time. Then while still chewing, reload and prepare to fire again. This is how Orville Redenbacher did it. You could look it up. God knows why there aren't instructions on the popcorn box.

When the movie is over, we still have half the huge container of popcorn left. It's not that my wife is no longer hungry, it's that her arm is killing her.

We take the popcorn home and the next evening watch old reruns of *Bonanza*. I hate that show, but I'm not saying anything. When Mary Ellen gets angry, that right arm packs quite a wallop.

Deep Trouble

Most of the wives in my neighborhood will do something for their husbands that Mary Ellen won't do. Maybe it was her upbringing. Maybe she just gets cold feet.

She won't shovel snow.

I walked out on my front porch to get the newspaper the morning after the storm that pelted central Indiana the week of Christmas. Sure enough, there were Julie, Angie, Kelly, and Nancy out there pushing the snow shovel, clearing their driveways, and having so much fun. I grabbed my shovel and joined in the party.

"Are you doing okay?" screamed Julie. "Where's Mary Ellen?"

"Oh, she's in the house probably cleaning the chimney or painting our crawl space. It's my turn to shovel snow."

Where was Mary Ellen? She was in our warm, toasty

kitchen—that's where she was. I couldn't stand it anymore. I was so angry, I stormed into the house. But
not before I dusted the snow off my gloves, took off
my wet boots, and hung my damp coat up in the
bathroom. I didn't want to tick her off before I gave
her a piece of my mind.

"Mary Ellen, did you know that I'm out there shoveling snow and I have a minor heart condition?"

"I know that, Dick. How selfish are you? While
you're out there playing in the snow, gossiping with
all the neighborhood women, I'm inside this hot
kitchen trying to find a low-fat holiday recipe to meet
your sausage obsession."

I never did ask her why she won't shovel. I was
afraid she'd assume it was important to me. This
couldn't be further from the truth. If she started shoveling snow, that would jeopardize our relationship by
altering the delicate balance between my wife's inde-
pendence and her femininity.

Of course, if she really wanted to shovel snow, I
wouldn't stop her.

When I decided to marry Mary Ellen, I guess it didn't
matter. I mean, after all, she was intelligent, beautiful,
sensitive, and caring. It was all a man could want. I
guess I just assumed that if push came to shove, she'd
shovel snow. And I bet if I had a really bad back problem and the snow was really deep, I bet she would
shovel then.

Sometimes I watch those other women shoveling and I actually find it kind of unattractive. I mean, they're wearing layers of old ratty sweat pants and big puffy coats and work boots. Of course, I wouldn't have to watch. And when Mary Ellen was finished, she could just freshen up and join me in front of the fire.

I actually think it's rather chauvinistic for a man to make his wife shovel snow. Of course, on the other hand, it's chauvinistic for a man to assume that a woman can't or won't shovel snow, so I guess I should at least ask her.

Maybe she really wants to shovel snow but is afraid I wouldn't let her. I'm sure that's it.

I'd even buy her a snowblower, just to show her I care and that I'm behind her 100 percent. But who am I kidding? Mary Ellen won't do snow. What's wrong with her, anyway? My friend, Jeff—his wife shovels snow. He was over the other day and asked me why Mary Ellen never shovels snow. I was as honest with him as I could be.

"I don't know, Jeff. I never really thought about it."

Waste Not, Want Not

So what are you going to do with your tax refund check? Everything I read says that if you are a good American and want to help the economy you will spend it, not save it. I find this concept very difficult to understand.

How in heaven's name do I know if I spent it or saved it? When I first got the check in the mail, I deposited it. I hope that's okay. Or does that mess things up for the economy and tick off Alan Greenspan? Do I have to go directly to Best Buy, sign the back of the check, and go home with a new DVD player? Where are the government guidelines when you need them?

My wife, who is quite the patriot, was very concerned about this. "What are we going to do with that two hundred dollars we received from President Bush?" she asked.

"Well, we're going to New York to see my mother. We could take her out to dinner."

"That's a bad idea."

"I thought you liked my mother."

"That's not what I mean. You were going to take your mother out to dinner anyway, so it doesn't count. If you really want to end that deficit, you'd have to take a stranger's mother out to dinner."

"Okay, we'll see a show on Broadway."

"Once again, you were going to do that anyway. It doesn't help the economy unless you buy something that you would not have bought if it weren't for the refund."

"Hold on here, Mary Ellen. How does George Bush know if I planned to take my mother to see *The Producers* on Broadway or not? How does the government know if I use the two hundred bucks to pay my lawn care company, buy pink satin leisure pants, or go out and spend it foolishly on food? In fact, how do I know what I spent it on? When I put the check in the bank, all that money just gets shmushed all together."

"Do you want to help the economy or not, Dick?"

"Yes, Mary Ellen. What should we do?"

"Okay, one more time. We need to buy something that we would not have bought if it were not for the two hundred dollars."

"You mean we should waste the money."

"Exactly. I'm glad ECON 101 has finally sunk in after thirty-five years."

"How about a new set of golf clubs? I just bought a new set, and therefore, I don't need a new set, so that way we're adding to the economy."

"Do you always think that selfishly, Dick? Why can't I ever buy something I don't want? Why is this always about you?"

"This is like *The Twilight Zone*. What do you NOT want?"

"I have always not wanted a beautiful silk scarf."

"You have? I mean you haven't? Look, Mary Ellen, I think we if are going to buy something that you never wanted, it has to be something that you would-n't have bought, even if you wanted it."

"You're making a good point. Tell you what. You take the two hundred dollars and buy me something for my birthday."

"How does that help?"

"In twenty-five years, you've never bought me any-thing I wanted."

Very Spatial Relationships

My wife is smarter than I am. She has, for most of our marriage, made more money than I do. She is far better looking and makes a better parent.

I wanted to tell you this up front because I'm going to make fun of her now and I don't want you think I'm a total jerk. As you'll see, I'm still not taking any chances.

This all started a few weeks ago when I was driving Mary Ellen's car and noticed that in six months she had gone exactly the number of miles allotted to her on the lease. Pleased we had made the right consumer choice, I used the circumstance to initiate some lively marital patter.

"Mary Ellen, guess how many miles you've driven since you got the car in August?" I asked.

"Heavens, I don't know. If I had to guess, eight hundred miles."

"Eight hundred miles? You've had the car for six months. You've driven twenty miles round-trip to work every day, five days a week for six months. How can you say eight hundred miles?"

"Well, you forgot to count shopping. That's why I guessed so high."

(My wife has an MBA, she's been a vice president of a major hospital, and her IQ is twenty points higher than mine. Okay, back to making fun of her...)

I began to realize that Mary Ellen has no sense of distance, speed, or time. I don't think most women do. A few examples:

"Mary Ellen, how far is it from New York to California?"

"I'll say fifty thousand miles."

"That's not even close."

"Well, don't go by my odometer. It was six thousand miles off on my trip to work."

"Let's try it another way. If you got in the car in New York and drove straight to California, how long would it take?"

"In months?"

"Months? We could travel from New York to L.A. in less than a week."

"Not if we stop in Vegas. What's the big rush?"

(My wife dresses better than I do, has better manners, understands movies, and speaks German.)

"Mary Ellen, how far is it from the earth to the moon?"

"Not a clue. I'll say five million miles."

Wow, I bet that even got a wince from Carl Sagan. "Actually, about 240,000 miles."

"I think these are trick questions. Do you mean as the crow flies?"

(My wife graduated in the top 10 percent of her class. She has perfect skin.)

"Okay, one more chance. If you get this answer within a million miles, I'll buy you an expensive candlelight dinner. How far is it around the earth at the equator?"

"Now, that has to be a million miles."

"No, but you did just describe Christopher Columbus's recurring nightmare. It's actually twenty-five thousand miles."

"My, it IS a small world. I thought that was just a Walt Disney expression. By the way, I won the bet."

(Beautiful figure, very sensitive...)

"One more chance to redeem yourself. How fast does light travel?"

"Hmmm. Well, you say California is three thousand miles away and my job is ten miles from the house and the moon is 240,000 miles from earth and the equator is twenty-five thousand miles around. Keeping that in mind, I'd say light travels 186,000 miles per second."

"I'm absolutely dumbfounded! That is correct. To be exact, it's 186,240 miles per second."

"Oooh, it got faster."

(She has great hair. And is very forgiving. I hope.)

Safe at Home

My wife's eyes glazed over, some drool came out of the side of her mouth, and her head was thrown back against the car seat.

No, this was not a vegetative state she had entered; she was listening to me talk about baseball.

We were on our way to the airport last week. Mary Ellen and Brett had taken scuba diving lessons and were headed for the Grand Cayman Islands. I told my wife that due to work, I did not have time to take the required certification test. I told my friends it was because I was too preoccupied with my skydiving lessons. And I told my son that I wanted to save the money so he could go to a better college. That's about all the lying I am capable of in a week.

The fact is that I am a huge baseball fan and didn't

want to miss the World Series. See, the truth will always come out eventually.

My wife, who bought my first story, was kinda feeling guilty, so she tried to make conversation in the car.

"Who is winning the World Games?"

"It's the World Series, and it's tied, two games apiece."

"Why do they play so many games? Why not play just one big one like the Super Game?"

"It's the Super Bowl. It's different with football."

"Why?

"It's hard to explain; just trust me."

"Which group are the Yankees in?"

"Not groups, leagues. American and National."

"Who decides who goes in what league?"

"It's hard to explain."

"Why should that be hard to explain? L.S. Ayres, Saks, and Kohl's are in different leagues. Any fan of shopping knows this. Shall I explain the difference?"

"NO, please. I give up. The American League has a DH, a designated hitter."

"Huh?"

"That means that the pitcher does not bat. Someone bats for him."

"That doesn't seem very fair to the pitcher."

"The pitcher doesn't care."

"Well, if he doesn't care, he shouldn't be playing. Can't they find people who do care?"

"Yes, Dear."

"Why do the umpires wear black?

"I have no idea. That sounds like a fashion question. Maybe you can field that one. HA HA!"

"Gee, Dick. I thought you knew baseball. Say, why do they call it a strike when the guy doesn't strike it, but in bowling they call it a strike when he does?"

"I don't know."

"Any why are there four balls and only three strikes?"

"I don't know. Hey, this is starting to sound like a Bob Newhart routine."

"Can you explain anything in baseball, Dick?"

"Sure. I can explain the infield fly rule."

"How exciting. Go for it."

"Okay! An infield fly is a fair fly ball (not including a line drive or an attempted bunt) which can be caught by an infielder with ordinary effort, when first and second, or first, second, and third bases are occupied, before two are out and..."

"ZZZZZZZZZZZZZzzzzzzzzzzzz..."

Whoa! Mary Ellen, you fell asleep. That is really very bad."

"Why?"

"Well, your falling asleep shows you really don't care, but more important, you're the one driving."

So, off my family went on a fabulous vacation. Days filled with fun and relaxation. In case you were scuba diving with my wife and son, the Miami Marlins won the World Series in seven games.

Sonny Days

My wife went away on a business trip for a week and left me alone with my seventeen-year-old son, Brett. She told me it was a chance for Brett and me to bond. The worst nightmare I ever had was about bonding—and a tube of Krazy Glue. I was nervous about this new experience.

In order to make me feel more comfortable, Mary Ellen gave me a detailed list of do's and don'ts. If I was unsure about anything, she told me, I was to consult the list. Everything—yes, everything—was in alphabetical order. For example:

- **B:** Bedtime (You both need to do this every night. Do not skip a night.)
- **D:** Dishes (Wash after each meal in dishwasher. Do not mix dishes and underwear in same load.)

- **M:** Meals (To be eaten while seated—not in the car, and not standing at the sink. Space them out over the day.)
- **V:** Vacuum Cleaner: (About three feet tall, with a long bag attached to it and a hose coming out the side. I don't expect you to use it, but I didn't want it to scare you if you opened the closet by mistake.)
- **X:** Xylophone (It's the only word I know with the letter X. You may play one while I am gone.)

What a sense of humor, huh?

I do love my son very much, but this was going to be the first time I had ever spent a week with him completely alone. I remember the first time I ever spent seven days and nights in a row with my wife. It went pretty well, but the next thing I knew, it was twenty-five years later and we were still living in the same house. This is not my intention with Brett. I need his room for an office some day.

That first morning, Brett and I had breakfast together in the kitchen. I watched as Brett ate a bowl of ice cream and a can of ravioli. I wondered if this was permissible.

"Brett, I don't think you are allowed to eat that stuff for breakfast when Mom is home."

"Probably not, Dad. Are you enjoying your cigar?"

I decided to let the ravioli and ice cream slide.

After about an hour of staring at each other during breakfast, my son finally said, "So what are we going to do, Dad?"

"Guy things, Brett. Guy things."

"You mean, like with girls? Aren't you too old for that?"

"I am not too old. I'm just not allowed. There's a big difference. We could play a computer game together."

"Okay, Dad, do you want to play Total Annihilation Kingdoms, Nerf Arena Blast, or Blood Wake?"

"No Pac-Man, huh?"

"Not in my lifetime."

"Brett, I have an idea. Let's you and I get some camping equipment, pack up the car, drive down to southern Indiana, and spend some time together."

"Dad, I don't want to hurt your feelings, but if we're just going to stare at each other like this, I'd rather be near a fridge and a flush toilet."

I tried not show it, but I liked the way the kid was thinking.

Well, I'm proud to say that Brett and I got through the week. We played racquetball, went out to dinner together, and spent time talking. By the way, I'm also going away for a few days in July. I will also leave Mary Ellen an alphabetical list of do's and don'ts. But my list will be completely different from hers.

Except maybe for that xylophone thing.

Meet the Napsters

Last Saturday something happened that made me very proud of my family and I want to share it with you.

It was about three in the afternoon and my son had just come home from his first day at his new job as a bag boy at Marsh Supermarket, my wife had just gotten back from a massage and a haircut, and I had finished playing eighteen holes of golf.

What was I proud of? Everyone took a nap. Right in the middle of the day. Other people in the neighborhood were mowing their lawns, cleaning out their garages, playing baseball with the kids, washing their cars. But the Wolfsies were all asleep, sacked out on a couch, a chaise lounge, and a king-sized bed. Do I know how to pick a family, or what?

I just wish I could have been awake to fully enjoy it. If I had not been napping myself, I would have run around the neighborhood bragging, "My whole family is taking a nap! My whole family is taking a nap!" Bellowing "Two out of three people in my family are taking a nap!" would have taken a bit of the shine off my bravado.

Of course, my son and wife are not experienced nappers. They have not spent the years I have perfecting the art of the timely snooze. My wife has never slept through Paris on a bus or dozed through an entire baseball game (and I was sitting right behind the catcher). My son has never fallen asleep at his own surprise birthday party or in the classroom (I was teaching grammar that day). They are novice nappers. But I was thrilled that there was hope. Here it was, Saturday afternoon, a gorgeous day begging every family in the neighborhood to come outside and bask in the fresh air. And all the Wolfsies were sleeping.

Of course, there are some drawbacks to amateur napping. When my wife awakens, she apologizes for her lapse, wonders out loud if she may have been bitten by something, and then spends the next three hours in a Roseanne-sized snit.

My son awakens from a nap in much the same way, but a teenage snit is unique. My wife's snits are Oscar material; the category is "Best Short Film." Brett once got up grumpy from a nap when he was fourteen and we're hoping it wears off before he leaves for college. A teenage snit is not a sitcom; it's a mini-series.

I see you nodding your head.

Later that day, we all went out to a movie and I watched other families interacting after the film. I imagined what they might have been doing all day: riding bikes, taking a walk together, visiting grandparents, having a picnic. Whatever it was, it didn't compare to what the Wolfsies had done that day.

You may think we wasted the afternoon. That we squandered valuable time, frittered it away, by dozing off at three in the afternoon.

You are entitled to your opinion. But I'm not going to lose any sleep over it.

Ghost of Christmas Present

Because Christmas is such a gay season, I have adopted a "Don't Ask, Don't Tell" approach to the holidays.

Wow, I better explain that.

As I have reported in the past, this is the traditional time of year when my wife starts asking the same question, over and over and over again:

"What do you want for Christmas?"

I have tried to take the same intellectual approach to this question that I have to other queries in our marriage. For example:

"Dick, what do you want for dinner?"

"I don't know."

"Dick, where should we go on vacation?"

"I don't know."

"Where did you park the car?"

"I don't know."

"Dick, what were you thinking?"

"I don't know."

"I'm going to Marsh. What do you want?"

"Miller Genuine Draft, nachos, salsa, summer sausage, and mint chocolate chip ice cream."

Hey, a man has to have some convictions.

Finally, my wife put her foot down. She told me that she will no longer accept this answer and that if I didn't get it together it would be the end of what some people who don't know us very well have called a perfect marriage.

"Okay, Dick, here's your chance to avoid divorce court. What do you want for Christmas?"

"I don't care."

"Hey, I'm impressed. Who would have thought at your age you could go from ignorance to apathy with such grace? I misjudged you."

"Look, Mary Ellen, if I really needed something, I'd have already bought it for myself. And if I don't really need it, you won't buy it for me."

"That's ridiculous. What do you want?"

"I'd like one of those cell phones that takes photos."

"Dick, that's a brilliant use of the precious money we need for Brett's college education. Why not invest the money directly in ENRON?"

"Okay, okay. How about a pair of socks? I'm out of matching socks."

"Well, if it isn't Mr. Excitement? You can buy socks

yourself. Get in the spirit, Dick. You were more fun when you didn't care and didn't know."

"What do you suggest, Mary Ellen?"

"Look, this is getting us nowhere. Just to make things move along, let's go back to me for a moment. I'll give a hint and see if you can pick up on it. This will be so much fun."

"Great! One hundred old issues of *Cosmo* on the coffee table with, 'how-to' tips and this is what you come up with for fun?"

"Yes. Here goes. I am reading a book. I am finished with the book. I look bored."

"OKAY! I got it. You want a new book to read."

"Geez, Dick, what fun would this game be if it were that obvious? No, I am bored. I need something to do. I better get in my car and go to a movie. Oh dear, my car is six years old. It sure would be great to have a new car. See how the game works?"

"Boy, do I feel stupid. Okay, let me try. I am watching football. I am thirsty. There is no brew in the fridge. I'm thinking that if I had a year's supply of Rolling Rock I wouldn't have to run out every Saturday night and get beer. Have you picked up on the hint?"

"I didn't know you wanted a new pair of warm gloves. Why didn't you just say so?"

Next year I'll mention to my wife that my golf clubs are a bit old. I hope she picks up on the hint. I desperately need a new wallet.

My Son, the Spamster

All of us are bothered by pesky e-mails known as spam. As I am sure you know, the SPAM people are very unhappy about this terminology. The SPAM people take their product very seriously and do not want it confused with something undesirable that you want to put in your trash bin.

I am continually deluged with electronic offers that make even a New Yorker blush. I don't know how these people got my e-mail address, but considering the nature of some of these products, I figure it must be some guy I used to shower with in high school gym class.

The best spam scam is a request from the sender to help reclaim money for some guy in Nigeria. Apparently he has a bank account in Switzerland and is having trouble transferring his money from his second cousin's estate in America. He wants my help to do this and I have to send him five grand so that ultimately he'll send me 5 percent of his money, which is about ten million dollars. I mean, how can you refuse an offer like that? The messages all start something like this:

> **I am Dr. Anya Duruoha, the esteemed Bank Manager of Diamond Bank of Nigeria, Lagos Branch. I have urgent and very confidential business proposition for you....**

I'd like to know who falls for this because I have an entire storage unit filled with unsold Dick Wolfsie books I would love to pawn off (I mean, sell) to some patsy (I mean, literary gourmet) who loves to read.

This last month I responded to all of the Nigerian messages requesting my financial help by pasting the sender's e-mail address into the spam mail forms to request information about herbal Viagra. I think these people just need something to keep them busy.

Recently, I found a Web site for aspiring spammists, including those interested in exploiting the Nigerian letter. A course was even being offered with the following topics:

- The effectiveness of using all UPPERCASE characters.
- "Are twenty million e-mails a day too many?"

- Cell phone text messaging: can it work?
- Grammatical errors: what's the optimal number?

My son, who spends a great deal of time on the computer and is very unhappy with his allowance, apparently found this Web site. I found this letter on his computer ready to be sent out.

Dear Person of Some Kindness,

My father is a person of great meanness who gives an allowance to me of very little worth. Please be it so nice of you to help me buy the food that I eat each day so that I have not to beg in the streets. I am not a person of great size, so even a donation of amounts of little size would make me a teenager of great happiness.

I live in tiny community of little value called Geist. Just twenty-five years ago there was not even running water in village and no roads. Now we are of too many people. I go to school each day in pants too big and must eat food that is of unhealthiness after standing in long line. Then I must come home in bus with other children to house of meaness.

> **Please to send small fortune to me so that I may live like other children who do not have father who gives allowance of so little.**
>
> **Brett of Geist**

You'll be pleased to know that I caught him just before he sent it out. It's a good thing. You were on the list. And I know what a softie you are.

Base Behavior

Did you read the story about the father and son who attended a professional baseball game together and in the fifth inning rushed the field and beat the pulp out of the first base coach?

One of the excuses offered by the father was that the first base coach was making obscene gestures. Had these guys never been to a ball game? That's what a first base coach is paid to do.

Finger in the air, hand on your butt: Lay down a bunt.

Finger toward your nose, hand between your legs: Take the next pitch.

I'm always looking for something to do with my fifteen-year-old son, so the idea of getting together on a beautiful afternoon and attacking a coach is the kind of creative activity that can make the male bond even stronger.

It is tough to find cool things to do with kids nowadays and no father wants to be called a square, so maybe we shouldn't come down too hard on this guy—although he had no problem coming down really hard on the first base coach.

I'm sure that this father had been unsuccessful at getting his son to the ballet or symphony and was kinda put out by the youngster's anti-opera feelings. I'm sure the father's suggestion to beat up a first base coach was a sort of last-ditch effort to find some activity the two could enjoy together. Let's cut the father some slack here.

And where was the mother? This is so typical of men today; Dad finally came up with a fun idea for a Sunday afternoon and he never mentioned it to Mom. She was probably home doing the dishes, knitting socks, or working on her left jab. Then she turned on the TV, only to discover that her family was out pummeling a perfect stranger and she wasn't invited to come along. And you wonder why women get depressed.

I think we should consider similar activities that would encourage fathers and sons to become even closer.

Father-and-Son Carjacking

A car, a dad, and his son. What could be more American, more apple pie? And sometimes Dad should let Junior drive, assuming he's of legal age. Letting a boy steal a car without a valid license is, well, setting a bad example.

Father-and-Son Light-Bulb Snatching

A great way to get better acquainted that teaches life skills like sleight of hand, misdirection, and concealment. Don't underestimate the value of petty crimes when it comes to your kids. There's a lesson around every corner. And on every ceiling.

Father-and-Son Shoplifting

What a wonderful way to spend a Sunday. Just the guys out at the local Wal-Mart stuffing their pockets with loot from the jewelry department. You can teach your son the value of being a smart consumer and show him how even a run-of-the-mill shoplifter does better than a highly trained Wal-Mart greeter.

Father-and-Son Public Indecency

There is no better way to bond with your number one son than being caught in a public area without your shirt and pants. A boy may forget the week his family took him to Disneyland, but spending a night buck-naked in the slammer with your father is a memory that never fades.

I think the most important lesson here is to be available to your kids. We are all busy, but it is important to give our kids time. In this case, I think the father will also get some time. I'd guess six months to a year.

Being a Good Sport

I'm not a huge sports fan. Compared to other guys, I'm just a casual observer who enjoys the intricacies of each game. I'm not addicted to football, obsessed with basketball, passionate about baseball, or compulsive about hockey. I do sleep with my golf clubs, but that's just a security issue. Why, if it weren't for remote controls and nachos, I could probably go an entire Saturday afternoon without watching three sports events in a row.

My wife has absolutely zero interest in sports. Nada. Nothing. When we first were thinking of getting married, I asked Mary Ellen what her idea of fun would be on a lazy Sunday afternoon. When she looked at me and said, "a game would be fun," I knew I had the perfect woman. Now she claims that she said, "I'm game for some fun," which makes me wonder if wishful thinking on my part led to the misunderstanding. I also think that when she batted her eyelids, that confused me.

The biggest problem my wife has with sports is that the games seem to go on forever. Mary Ellen's mindset is based on old movies. At two o'clock on a Sunday afternoon, George Peppard and Audrey Hepburn meet. By four thirty they are in love. Done. Finished. No umpire or referee comes out and says, "Let's see that embrace one more time. Sorry, illegal use of the hands. We'll have to replay that kiss and reset the clock."

Because movies wrap things up in neat time frames, my wife expects the same from sports. Here are a few exchanges we have had during sporting events.

World Series

"What are you watching, Dick?"

"Baseball, Mary Ellen. The World Series."

"Again with the World Series. Isn't this like the seventh game in a row you've watched? Does this thing ever end? Can't you miss just this one little teensy-weensy game and paint the garage?"

"This is the last game."

"You said that after games three, four, five, and six. After all this time, I'd have thought you understood baseball a little bit better."

The Superbowl

"What are you watching, Dick?"

"Football. The Superbowl."

"How much longer is this going to last?"

"Five minutes left before it's over."

"You said that fifteen minutes ago."

"Fifteen minutes ago, there were six minutes left."

"And I thought I was bad in math. Look, I'm going shopping. I'll be gone about twenty minutes. Football time."

Cricket

One day while channel-surfing, I came upon a cricket match in England. Just then my wife walked in.

"Now what are you watching?"

"Oh, I think it's cricket. I'll change the channel."

"No, there's a night watchman at bat."

"What?"

"Yes, Dick, a night watchman is a batsman in cricket who comes in to bat out of order toward the end of a day's play in order to 'protect' better batsmen. To elucidate, the batting order in an inning is usually arranged with two specialist openers who begin the innings, then the rest of the batsmen go in order of skill, best to worst. The job of the openers is to bat for a while against the new ball. A brand new ball is very hard and bouncy, and fast bowlers can use this to great advantage and can often get batsmen out. Geez, Dick, don't you know anything about sports?"

That's the end of this essay. I couldn't think of anything clever to say then, either.

Home Sweet Home

As I was riding my exercise bike this week, I heard something snap. When you are exercising at more than fifty-five (that's years, not miles per hour) and you hear something snap, you immediately fear that some aspect of future activity has been compromised. It's either the end of golf, sex, or shoveling snow. I was hoping for number three, but my wife says otherwise. That's all the information you're getting.

Turns out it wasn't my back, or hamstring, or shoulder. It was my exercise bike. Can you imagine? This is really ironic because I have never demanded very much from my exercise equipment.

I put a couple of thousand miles on my Suzuki SUV every month and never have a problem. My fridge door is opened about three hundred times a day and has never failed me. My electric toothbrush has been in some pretty tight situations but it never falters. If it did, I'd just go manual for a few days.

But this exercise machine thing has got me in a bad mood. My workouts are really more style than substance. I put on a pair of designer sweats, a clean T-shirt, and my Nikes, turn on the TV and casually spin the pedals on my Tunturi recumbent bike until I break into a glisten, at which time I turn down the tension in the wheel. I think it was Mark Twain who once said, "There's no profit in getting tired." I've always loved that man.

So I had a choice. Join a health club at about $120 a month or buy a new recumbent bike for about $2,000. Whenever I need advice in the financial area, I call my mother. Joan is the world's cheapest person, but that's only because my father has gone to a better place. Or as he used to say, "a less expensive place."

I decided to broach the subject indirectly. I knew that Mom was in great shape for someone sixty-five, and she's eighty-seven.

"So Mom, are you keeping active?"

"Of course. I walk three miles every day."

"Isn't it kind of cold for you? It's the middle of winter."

"Oh, I walk indoors."

"Indoors? You bought an expensive treadmill?"

"Of course not. Attic, kitchen, hallway, master bedroom, your brother's old room. Then attic, kitchen, hallway, master bedroom, your brother's old room. Then basement, kitchen, hallway, master bedroom, your brother's old room. Attic, kitchen...."

"Okay, I get the picture..."

"What picture? I haven't walked a hundred yards yet."

"Wait a second. Don't you walk in my old room?"

"It's still a mess."

"Doesn't it get a little boring doing the same route over and over?"

"Well, I don't meet a lot of new people if that's what you mean. But I see things."

"You see things? Like what?"

"A table I never noticed before, a new plant. I have a lovely home. All I ever did was complain. Now I'm enjoying it. Come over, we'll take a walk."

"Can't you walk in the mall like a normal senior citizen?"

"Well, when your father was alive I was a mall walker, but I did it at two in the afternoon and it cost your dad about two thousand dollars a month so he took away my sneakers. I also go on the StairMaster every day."

"You bought a StairMaster? Now those are expensive."

"Ours came with the house fifty years ago. It's conveniently located and you can get down to the basement with it. I also swim at home every day for about a mile."

"Where do you swim? You don't have a pool in that tiny house."

"Well, of course, I do. Ever since the flood, the StairMaster goes right down to it."

Calendar Girl

It is always interesting to me when I find out something new about my mother. Joan is eighty-seven and lives in New York. I have known her fifty-eight years so you'd think that she'd be pretty much out of surprises. Never sell your mother short. In fact, in today's market, I wouldn't even sell a mother.

I think most of us feel that way about our mothers. But sometimes we hear things we don't expect from them....

"Well, dear, I thought you should know that I am now almost 100 percent sure that Edgar was your father."

"This probably just slipped my mind, Eric, but have I ever mentioned your identical twin that we gave up for adoption?"

"It wasn't 'til your father died that I really learned how to kiss."

Okay, my mother has never said stuff like this, but the other day in our weekly Sunday phone conversation I did learn something new. Apparently, my mother writes down everything on a calendar. I mean everything. She informed me that she didn't feel well, for the third Sunday in a row—and the twelfth Sunday this year that she was under the weather.

"I've not had a bad Tuesday all year," she told me.

"Do you keep track of stuff like that?"

"Sure. I have a calendar and every night before bed I write down how I felt that day. You don't do that?"

"No, I don't, Mom. Why do you do that?"

"Suppose someone asked me how I felt on June 8, 2001. Who would remember?"

"What do you write down?"

"I have a few key words I use: Great! Eh! Could be better! Don't ask! And, Oy! I put all that down after I record the weather."

"You put the weather down on the calendar also?"

"Of course. When people ask how I felt on June 8, I can't just say lousy. I want to say 'Lousy, but what a nice day.' Or maybe, 'Great, but what a storm.'"

"Okay, so read me November 3, 1999."

"Let's see. It says, Eh, three miles, cold, nothing, electric can opener, *An Affair to Remember*."

"I may regret this, but I need a translation."

"'Eh' is how I felt. 'Three miles' is how far I walked for exercise, and 'cold' is the weather."

"What does 'nothing' refer to?"

"None of your business. But this happens when you get older. And it's good to keep track."

"I'm afraid to ask. *'An Affair to Remember'*?"

"It's an old movie I watched, Mr. Nosey. If I don't write it down, I keep renting the same film."

"And finally, Mom, why 'electric can opener'?"

"Is this my son I am talking to? I always write it down when a new appliance comes in the house. TV, January 6, 1998; washing machine, February 8, 1987; dryer, June 4, 1986. If you don't write it down, how would you know?"

"God help me. Why do you do this?"

"Let's say I have a friend over. She says, 'What a neat toaster.' I can say, 'Yes, I've had it seventeen years. Still toasts.' I don't have a great deal to brag about, you know."

"Well, Mom, I must say that this is all news to me. I have talked to you every Sunday for the last twenty-five years and you have never mentioned any of it."

"Not every Sunday. You missed the first Sunday of April 1998, the second Sunday in July 2000, and the fourth Sunday in March 2002."

"How long have you been writing this stuff down?"

"Since the day I got married."

"How long ago was that again?"

"Heavens, I don't have a clue."

Part 4

*Shear*iously Speaking

(Gentle-as-a-Lamb Observations)

Record Comedy

Where have all the great comedians gone? There's no record of them.

And no CDs.

Or DVDs.

Last week I gave a speech on the development of humor in America. I have always been intrigued by funny people. As a kid in New York, I often went to the same Neil Simon play several times a month. I enjoyed watching people laugh. I still do.

I've been trying to find a few more recordings of my favorite comics from back in the '60s and '70s. I went to one of those superstores.

"I'm looking for something by Shelly Berman."

"Never heard of her. What group does she sing with?"

"He's a he, not a she. He's not a singer and he's not with a group. He's a comedian."

"Everyone's a comedian. Sorry, we don't carry humor."

I pretty much got the same story everywhere I went. A few places had a Woody Allen disc. I found one Robert Klein. And one Barnes & Noble had three different CDs of the *2,000-Year-Old Man*. That's like finding three pearls in the same oyster.

I found an Internet site called laugh.com. The man who answered at their toll-free number said the site was barely staying afloat. The humor business, he said, is not what it used to be. What a shame. Amazon.com had a pretty good selection, but I feel the same way about a CD as I do a book. I want to browse in a store, pick the product up, see if it sends me any vibes. (I'm serious.)

In my personal collection I have old radio shows of Jack Benny, Burns and Allen, and Edgar Bergen and Charlie McCarthy, to name a few. These are knee-slapping shows. I am not old enough to remember the original broadcasts, but I am smart enough to know classic writing when I see and hear it. Old radio shows created characters while vaudeville comedy was dependent on the written joke, since oftentimes this was the first and only time you'd see that performer. But people grew to know Jack Benny and Gracie Allen, just like they know the characters in the modern sitcoms like *Friends, Cheers,* or *Frasier.*

And the great comedians spoke to their audience. Jack Benny, for example, joked about his own cheapness and appealed to a society that had been through a depression and was concerned about money themselves. The Marx

Brothers played to a new wave of immigrants trying to fit in. Jerry Seinfeld appealed to a '90s society chock-full of self-absorbed individuals, much like the characters in the show. But Jerry, like Jack, gave the laughs to other people. True comedians don't have to say funny things; they create an environment for people in which to laugh. Jerry and Jack should be sold at music stores. Maybe even appliance stores.

Mel Brooks put me in tears the other night as I listened to his classic *2,000-Year-Old Man*. Not a dirty word (except where absolutely necessary), not mean-spirited. Just a marvelous celebration of a slightly warped view of the past looking at it from the present. His two-thousand-year-old character has a Jewish accent, yet his observations are universal. But the transcript of a two-thousand-year-old man routine would not strike you as funny. It's all about Brooks's attitude and delivery. Mel Brooks is a funny person. His CD should be in music stores. And in grocery stores. Why not?

I listened to as many tapes as I could find for my lecture: Robert Klein, Rodney Dangerfield, Woody Allen, Abbott and Costello, George Carlin. Jackie Mason's lampoon of Starbucks coffee is a classic. It should be in Target. And Starbucks, for that matter.

It wasn't easy finding all this stuff. The good news is I still do have a Bob Newhart album and a Shelly Berman album in my basement.

The bad news is I don't have a record player.

Goodbye, Johnny

Johnny Carson is gone. It's time to remember a man who changed the habits of a nation. This is the second time he has left us. We'll miss him all over again.

Stars like Milton Berle, Jack Paar, and Steve Allen forged a new medium in the '50s, but it was Carson who fully understood TV's potential and its limits. Television was truly invented for Johnny Carson.

He didn't create the monologue, but he fine-tuned it to such a pitch that it was pure music. He didn't just have the right lyrics, he also had the perfect harmony. And when he did hit a sour note, you didn't care. Neither did Carson. You laughed about it together.

His comic timing was perfect, and in the spirit of Carson's hero, Jack Benny, Carson knew the value of silence, the comic effect of a wayward look, or the cocking of the head. On the first *Tonight Show* back in 1962, Carson was introduced by Groucho Marx, another great comic who knew the worth of a raised eyebrow. As I watched clips of Carson the last two days, I was struck at how many times his facial demeanor framed one of his classic ad-libs.

His humor was often self-deprecating, but he, like Will Rogers and Mark Twain, could throw a political dart and have it end in a belly laugh. His skewering of Richard Nixon during the Watergate hearings was probably the first ongoing daily televised satire of a developing political story. In an age before cable, Carson helped bring this scandal to the late-night viewer.

When Carson sat with a guest, you weren't listening to an interview, you were eavesdropping on a conversation. And you weren't the only one listening; Carson was listening—a rare trait among talk show hosts. Carson recognized the key to TV was to do the hard work before the show but make it look easy on-air. When I watched Carson talk to a guest (the famous and the not-so-famous), I realized the importance of making the guest the star. Oh, Carson always got his share of laughs, but he never stole the limelight; he just borrowed it for a second.

Carson could go from his comic opening monologue to an interview with Richard Nixon or Bobby Kennedy, then back to shtick as the mystical answer man, Carnac the Magnificent.

No one had ever made such difficult transitions before; none has done it as well since.

There was always a mystery about Johnny Carson. While his humor occasionally was personal, even spotlighting his three failed marriages, he never really let the viewer inside. His world was private except for the ninety minutes when he came out from behind the curtain. But at that moment you were invited into his living room and most people—in a world before VCRs and TiVo—didn't leave until the party was over ninety minutes later.

Carson's retirement was elegant. It was final and complete. No talk show appearances, no hawking products. He went out on top.

And it took two people to replace him.

Respect the Comedian

For hundreds of years, humor theorists have proposed that all humor is about feeling superior. That laughter comes from seeing others ridiculed. Hogwash. Sigmund Freud slipped when he contended that jokes are really repressed aggressive and sexual impulses that...oh, enough of this baloney.

Rodney Dangerfield is gone. And after eighty-two years, it's finally time to give this man some respect. He proved Freud wrong. And he made us laugh. I love that combination.

("My wife and I were happy for twenty years. Then we met.")

My love of Rodney began as a twenty-year-old growing up near New York City. I used to sneak into Rodney's nightclub in Manhattan...not for alcohol, but for a small shot of his quirky brand of humor. As soon as

Rodney walked on stage people began to laugh. When he said, "I don't get no respect," everyone applauded. This was early in his career, but already he had established a shtick that would make him an original.

At Dangerfield's, there was no cover, no minimum. Now *that's* respect for the customer.

(*"I asked my father if I could go ice skating on the lake. He told me to wait until it got warmer."*)

As a kid, I didn't think I got that much respect either, so I related to his self-deprecating one-liners. So did the audience. But the audience wasn't laughing because Rodney made them feel superior. They laughed because they identified with his plight.

(*"I was so ugly, when I was born, the doctor slapped my mother."*)

Dangerfield cut his comedy teeth in the Catskills, capitalizing on his slovenly appearance: portly, unattractive, bulging eyes, sweaty. He always wore a crumply white shirt and red tie. It was his visual trademark. Few other comedians had one. Not Bob Hope, not Jack Benny, not Don Rickles, not Jackie Mason.

(*"A girl called me and said, 'Come on over, nobody's home.' I went over. Nobody was home."*)

Dangerfield should get respect for another reason. He was never a great ad-libber, but he knew how to craft each joke for the perfect delivery. When I was the host of *Good Morning New York* on WABC in the '80s, I interviewed Rodney once. I asked him about one of his famous jokes…

("I worked in a pet store and people kept asking how big I'd get.")

"Did you write that joke?" I asked him, knowing that comedians often buy one-liners from others.

"I'm still writing it," he said with a wink. What a great answer.

("We were so poor in my neighborhood, the rainbow was in black and white.")

And he deserves respect for still another reason. Dangerfield had great admiration for the younger comics. He hired them at his club in New York. Many became stars, like Richard Lewis, Jim Carrey, and Jerry Seinfeld.

("I come from a stupid family. During the Civil War, my uncle fought for the West.")

How ironic. The very people who he claimed gave him no respect were the people who made him a star. Not a superstar. Just a man with a unique ability to make us laugh at ourselves, not because we felt superior to Rodney but because down deep inside, we know all of our collars are also just a little too tight.

Elephant Jokes

Politically, I was not always a fan of Ronald Reagan, but I had great admiration for a man who instinctively understood the might and effectiveness of humor.

While some wit is used to hurt or demean others, the quintessential snappy remark is self-deprecating. This is especially true for those in power. It would be unseemly for a person like President Bush or President Clinton to make fun of others. People at the top need not ridicule; there is no humor in benefiting from an unfair advantage.

Ronald Reagan was probably not the quipster or ad-libber that John F. Kennedy was. But as I reflect on some of the wittier remarks that Reagan made, I marvel at how he innately knew how he was perceived and how a jab at himself would allay criticism and make him likable.

Marc Katz, a humor writer for Al Gore, had fun with his client, who once allowed himself to be rolled onto a stage by a UPS delivery man and had the host of the event sign for him like a package. It takes a certain amount of confidence and even courage to shoot yourself with a humorous barb. I admire that quality.

But back to Ronald Reagan. The former president recognized that humor was not just a way to campaign, it was an important technique in governing, as well. Reagan did not just use humor; he was truly, I believe, a man who embraced it as an integral part of life. Regardless of your political persuasions, you could not make this case for either of our candidates in the 2004 election. Bush and Kerry may, on occasion, say something funny. But they are not funny people. And they never will be. No matter how hard they try. Which is part of the problem.

Ronald Reagan was funny. Here are a few wonderful reminders:

- "The remark accusing me of having amnesia was uncalled for. I just wish I remembered who said it."

- "Things are busy at the White House. I've been burning the midday oil."

- "Hard work never killed anyone, but I'm not taking any chances."

- "I have left orders to be awakened in an emergency—even if I'm in a cabinet meeting."

- "I'm not worried about the deficit. It's big enough to take care of itself."

- "I've been around so long that I remember when a hot story broke, I yelled, 'Stop the chisel!'"

Great stuff. Not just great lines, but perfect material for diffusing what were the classic criticisms of Reagan: his age, his work ethic, and the deficit. Did it work? Don't expect a similar funeral for any of the more recent presidents.

President Reagan could, unlike most others, successfully make jokes with a touch of social commentary. That is easier to do when people like you despite your politics.

- "The taxpayer—that's someone who works for the federal government but doesn't have to take a civil-service exam."

- "Government's view of the economy could

be summed up in a few short phrases: If it moves, tax it. If it keeps moving, regulate it. And if it stops moving, subsidize it."

- "The nine most terrifying words in the English language are, 'I'm from the government and I'm here to help.'"

- "A recession is when your neighbor loses his job. A depression is when you lose yours. And recovery is when Jimmy Carter loses his."

- "I hope you're all Republicans" (to surgeons as he entered the operating room following his assassination attempt).

Now, don't get me wrong. I don't vote for a presidential candidate based on his sense of humor.

It's a good thing. Or I probably wouldn't vote at all.

The Doctor is "In"

This is the one hundredth anniversary of the birth of Theodore Geisel—better known as Dr. Seuss—and kids and parents all over the world are celebrating.

Why not? Dr. Seuss changed reading and the way it was taught.

To quote one pundit: He slew Dick and Jane.

I remember fifty years ago when Mrs. Morgan, my third grade teacher, read the very first Dr. Seuss book aloud to my class. *And to Think That I Saw It on Mulberry Street.*

The book had been rejected by publishers twenty-eight times. Seuss, who was told by his high school art teacher that he had no talent, persisted with his dream.

It's clearly Seuss's simplest book; no hidden agenda. Well, not really.

Not like *The Cat in the Hat*, where even as an

elementary school kid I wondered where the mother had gone. Was there some deeper symbolism there? At ten years old, I didn't give it much thought. Seuss's commentary in other books on the environment, prejudice, and even Nazi Germany was something I read about later, not as a kid.

But when Mrs. Morgan read *Mulberry Street*, I sat there mesmerized as Marco's imagination took him to places he had never actually gone. Each image was but a building block to a new, exciting layer in the fantasmagoric story he was weaving.

His tale was getting bigger. And better. But if he told this story to someone, it would be a lie.

To a kid like me who was already spending three days a week detained after school for an overactive imagination, I related to Marco's dilemma. Mrs. Hausman, my second grade teacher, had once written my mother and complained that "incessant word play was disruptive in class."

But back to Marco's fantasy. Where was the harm? Who does it hurt to live in a fantasy world...at least for a while? That's what I thought as a seven-year-old.

Marco knew when he got home his story wouldn't fly and chose not to face the scowl of a doubting father—although, ironically, it was his father who lectured him on being more observant in the first place.

I think Dr. Seuss wished Marco could have shared the fantasy with his dad. Then the two could have celebrated the value of a boy's vivid imagination.

"Was there nothing to look at, no people to greet?
Did nothing excite you or make your heart beat?"

"Nothing," I said, growing red as a beet,
"But a plain horse and wagon on Mulberry Street."

Unwittingly, Marco's father had stifled his son's imagination. As teachers and parents, we should guard against this. When I was a kid, if I said something funny at the dinner table, my dad would retreat to the bedroom so I would not see him laughing. Years later, my mother explained that he did not want to encourage behavior that was getting me into trouble at school.

Just before my father died in 1990, he admitted his little game. We laughed together about it. I wish we hadn't waited so long.

Books of Interest

Also by Dick Wolfsie

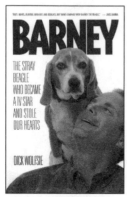

Barney: The Stray Beagle Who Became a TV Star and Stole Our Hearts
$14.99   Paperback
ISBN: 1-57860-167-3

Life in a Nutshell: A Nutty Look at Life, Marriage, TV and Dogs
$15.95   Paperback
ISBN: 1-57860-080-4

Dick Wolfsie's New Book
$12.95   Paperback
ISBN: 1-57860-197-5

Co-written with Gary Sampson, DVM

Dog Dilemmas: Simple Solutions to Everyday Problems
Part of the Pet Peeves series
$9.99   Paperback
ISBN: 1-57860-226-2

Cat Conundrums: Simple Solutions to Everyday Problems
Part of the Pet Peeves series
$9.99   Paperback
ISBN: 1-57860-227-0